The
WORST-CASE SCENARIO
Survival Handbook:
WORK

The
WORST-CASE SCENARIO
Survival Handbook:
WORK

By Joshua Piven and David Borgenicht
Illustrations by Brenda Brown

CHRONICLE BOOKS

SAN FRANCISCO

Copyright © 2003 by Quirk Productions, Inc.

Worst-Case Scenario™ and The Worst-Case Scenario Survival Handbook™ are trademarks of Quirk Productions, Inc.

Library of Congress Cataloging-in-Publication Data available.

ISBN: 0-8118-3575-8

Manufactured in Singapore

Typeset in Adobe Caslon, Bundesbahn Pi, and Zapf Dingbats

Designed by Frances J. Soo Ping Chow
Illustrations by Brenda Brown

A **QUIRK** Book
www.quirkproductions.com
Visit www.worstcasescenarios.com

Distributed in Canada by Raincoast Books
9050 Shaughnessy Street
Vancouver, British Columbia V6P 6E5

10 9 8 7 6 5 4 3

Chronicle Books LLC
85 Second Street
San Francisco, California 94105
www.chroniclebooks.com

WARNING

When a life is imperiled or a dire situation is at hand, safe alternatives may not exist. To deal with the worst-case work scenarios presented in this book, we highly recommend—insist, actually—that the best course of action is to consult a professionally trained expert. But because highly trained professionals may not always be available when the safety or sanity of individuals is at risk, we have asked experts on various subjects to describe the techniques they might employ in these emergency situations. THE PUBLISHER, AUTHORS, AND EXPERTS DISCLAIM ANY LIABILITY from any injury that may result from the use, proper or improper, of the information contained in this book. All the information in this book comes directly from experts in the situation at hand, but we do not guarantee that the information contained herein is complete, safe, or accurate, nor should it be considered a substitute for your good judgment, common sense, or regard for job security. And finally, nothing in this book should be construed or interpreted to infringe on the rights of other persons or to violate criminal statutes; we urge you to obey all laws and respect all rights, including property rights and employment rights, of others.

—The Authors

CONTENTS

Hard work never killed anybody,
but why take a chance?

—Charlie McCarthy
(Edgar Bergen, 1903–1978)

INTRODUCTION

Most people spend more than one-third of their adult waking lives on the job.

And during any given work week, usually Monday to Friday, you will spend half your awake time working—more than that, if you include commuting time (and a little less than that if you sleep on the job).

If you work in an office, this means you will most likely spend more time sitting in your desk chair than you will spend shopping, driving your car, playing with your dog, running errands, going to the movies, working out at the gym, playing golf, reading to your children, and eating *combined*. If your workplace is not an office, you'll spend just as much time there *and* you'll probably be surrounded by heavy machinery, dangerous chemicals, unpredictable environments, or incompetent co-workers. And everyone faces the risks imposed by a nightmare boss.

You spend so much time in the work environment, the odds are staggering that something is going to go wrong while you're there. Very wrong. Using an ergonomic chair or bending your knees when you lift something heavy is not going to be enough to keep you safe.

You need this book.

Work, to start with, isn't the greatest thing—that's why they call it *work*. But there's no sense in making it even worse by being unprepared and succumbing to physical, mental, social, and occupational

the worst-case scenario survival handbook: work

disasters. To keep you safe and productive in all the phases of your work life, we've created this indispensable handbook. After all, that's *our* job.

We've discovered that most people at work focus too much attention on too few problems and complaints: There are many more things that can get you than you realize.

From a job interview gone bad to a satisfying way to quit, from a deep-fryer burn to ways to sneak out of a meeting, from a necktie caught in a copy machine to expunging the nasty e-mail you sent, and from being locked in a walk-in freezer to retrieving a candy bar stuck in the lunchroom vending machine, this book will give you the tools necessary to survive and keep working. Sometimes you will be covering your own mistakes—restoring a shredded document, fixing a bad haircut, undenting the company car—other times you will be dealing with crises thrust upon you—a stockroom avalanche or the company picnic. In other instances, you will be turning your liabilities into advancement by disguising your tattoos, surviving an office romance, enhancing your stature, and starting a rumor. All the information in this book is geared toward helping you survive your workaday life, whether you're working behind the counter, behind the wheel, or behind a desk.

As with our other *Worst-Case Scenario Survival Handbooks,* we've consulted dozens of highly trained professionals to come up with clear, step-by-step instructions for emerging intact from the situation at hand. These experts—brain surgeons, human resources specialists, forklift operators, professional slackers, plumbers, photocopier technicians, lion tamers, escape artists, private investigators, and many others—all have one goal in mind: getting you though the on-the-job worst-case scenario so you can work another day.

—The Authors

CHAPTER I

THE INTERVIEW

HOW TO IDENTIFY A NIGHTMARE WORKPLACE

1 Interview at the beginning or end of the day.
Arrive early for your morning interview and observe the workers as they arrive. Slouching, pouting, and dejected expressions indicate low morale. Note whether workers acknowledge the receptionist with a smile and a greeting or are oblivious to the receptionist. With an interview at the end of the day, observe if large numbers of workers leave promptly at quitting time, which may indicate a bored, clock-watching staff. Large numbers of people working late, however, may indicate that employees are overworked and deadlines are unrealistic.

2 Examine the bathrooms.
Are the bathrooms clean? Is there enough toilet paper? Are paper towels strewn about the floor? Lack of attention to these small details may indicate a lack of respect for the workplace and lack of attention to larger details.

3 Monitor the air quality.
Does the work area have natural light and outside air? Is the environment quiet? Is the air too hot or too cold? Are there any rancid or chemical smells? Is smoke billowing from any vents or machinery? Are

Signs of a Troubled Workplace

slouching and pouting

staff leaves promptly at quitting time

how to identify a nightmare workplace

workers sniffing or sneezing frequently? All of these are indicators of poor air quality or a "sick" workplace.

4 Look for signs of a troubled workplace.
- Lack of personal photos on desks—only motivational images of rowers and bears catching salmon
- Droopy eyelids obscuring the whites of the workers' eyes
- Multiple sandwiches (partially eaten) and cans of soda at workstations
- Employees sleeping, doodling, or fist-fighting at meetings
- Employees with their foreheads on their desks, fists pounding the desktops
- Outdated or no-longer-manufactured candy in the vending machine
- Brown water in the cooler
- Flickering or humming fluorescent lights
- Music playing through speakers in the ceiling
- "Warning: Hazardous Waste" signs
- Groups of workers whispering
- Individual workers whispering to themselves
- Groups of workers silently praying
- Office layout based on slave ship rather than feng shui
- Carpet stains that could be coffee, could be blood

If you observe three or more of the above danger signs, you may have discovered a nightmare workplace.

5 Evaluate.
Is this the job for you?

HOW TO GET A JOB YOU'RE NOT QUALIFIED FOR

Fancy Restaurant

Restaurant interviews focus on your service experience, knowledge of standard service customs and procedures, and familiarity with a wide range of food items. You also are judged on your overall appearance and general demeanor.

Attire
Wear:
- Tuxedo

or

- White blouse with black skirt (below the knee)

Do Not Wear:
- Ripped jeans
- Facial hair (except a groomed mustache)
- Dark-colored nail polish
- Lots of jewelry (limit is a watch, a wedding band and/or engagement ring, and a pair of stud earrings)

Paraphernalia to Bring
- Table crumber
- Worm (waiter's corkscrew)
- Matches or a lighter

BUZZWORDS TO USE

- Cover (one person's dinner—derives from a single dinner plate with metal cover)
- Gooseneck (gravy boat)
- Eighty-sixed (the item is gone/finished)
- Bring-back (an unsatisfactory dish returned to the kitchen)
- Weeded (when you are attempting to serve too many tables at once)
- One fancy French wine appellation, perfectly pronounced

CRITICAL KNOWLEDGE

- American banquet trays should be carried in the left hand, leaving the right hand free to pick up service items and open doors. (Doors in restaurants in the United States swing out and have hinges on the right.) Your left hand should be flat, palm up, thumb toward your body, under the center of the bus tray, with the tray resting on your shoulder.
- You should be able to carry 10 covers at once.
- Stack the covers on the banquet tray as follows: One stack of two plates at each oblong end of the tray, one stack of three plates directly over your left shoulder, and one stack of three plates just beyond it.
- Hold cocktail trays at waist level, for beverages.
- Never put empty dishes and glassware together on the same banquet tray.

- Serve food from the left, drinks from the right. In the United States, all food items should be served from the left, using the left hand, left foot in toward the table. Drinks should be poured and items cleared from the right, using the right hand, right foot in. (French restaurants and exclusive hotels may use "modern French service," with all items served and cleared from the right.)
- Do not look at drinks as you carry them on a tray—it is easier to maintain a steady hand if you are not watching the liquids shift.
- Offer job references from out-of-town restaurants. Say, "I worked for years at Chez Louis in Chicago." If pressed for the name of a person, add, "Unfortunately, the restaurant never reopened after the fire and I don't know how to reach the owner/manager anymore."

CEO

Applying for a CEO job is a lengthy process and will require multiple interviews. Be prepared for several face-to-face meetings with the human resources department, senior management, and board members.

Attire
Wear:
- Navy or beige suit, white shirt, and a solid or wide-striped tie
  or

- Navy or beige jacket and skirt or a pantsuit or dress (for less conservative companies)
- Expensive-looking watch
- Shined shoes

Do Not Wear:
- Bow tie or clip-on necktie
- Loud-print blouse
- Open-toed shoes
- Pastels

Do Not:
- Remove your jacket during the interview
- Have dirty fingernails

Paraphernalia to Bring
- Leather portfolio
- Ultra-expensive fountain pen
- Cigar clipper
- Putter (collapsible)
- Credit cards and large bills—no coins or bills smaller than $20

Buzzwords to Use
- Gross margin (the difference between sales revenue and the cost of the goods sold)
- Book value (the value of all the assets)
- EBITDA (earnings before interest, taxes, depreciation, and amortization)
- Buy-in
- Buy-out

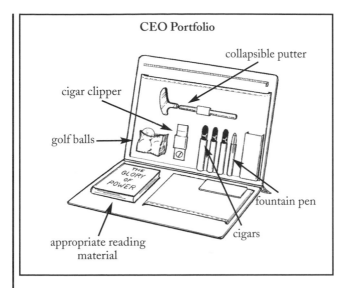

CEO Portfolio

- collapsible putter
- cigar clipper
- golf balls
- THE GLORY OF POWER
- fountain pen
- cigars
- appropriate reading material

- Re-conceptualize
- Re-energize
- Right-size

CRITICAL KNOWLEDGE

- Ask about the company's challenges over the next 6 to 12 months, its business plan or model, and whether it is in "growth" mode.
- Focus your questions on the business as a whole, the marketplace, or the global economy rather than on the details of the job.
- To prepare, read books on good grammar and writing style rather than business books. People are always more impressed with someone who communicates clearly, effectively, and correctly.

Use spell-checking software whenever you draft a cover letter or resume.

INSIDER TIP

- Be sure to ask about the number of stock options available to you, as well as their "strike price" (the price at which you can exercise them).
- When asked about your hiring strategy, say, "To hire people smarter than I am." Presidents like hearing this—it makes them trust you.
- Always negotiate for a higher salary and better benefits than offered—presidents will be more comfortable placing the business in the hands of a bulldog.

FORKLIFT OPERATOR

Driving a forklift requires specialized skills and lots of practice, so mention that you have operated a "fork" or "stacker" at many previous job sites.

ATTIRE
Wear:
- Clean T-shirt
- Work boots
- Baseball cap

Do Not Wear:
- Loafers or flip-flops
- Necktie
- Collared shirts other than flannel
- Short pants

Paraphernalia to Bring
- Lunch box/cooler
- Work gloves
- Cigarettes or chew
- Multi-purpose tool on belt

Buzzwords to Use
- Towmotor, high-low, stacker, truck (slang fork-lift names)
- Forks, carriage, mast/upright, load backrest (important parts of the forklift)
- Cage/DOG (for Driver's Overhead Guard)/ ROPS (pronounced "ropes," Roll-Over Protection Structure)

Critical Knowledge
- The primary fork controls on a forklift are the lift-lower, the tilt forward-back, and the side shifter.
- A fork has a transmission selector (forward, reverse, neutral), steering wheel, parking brake, and accelerator and brake pedals. Most units are now automatic, and these may also have a separate inching pedal to the left of the brake pedal that slips the transmission and moves the forklift very slowly. The inching pedal may also be built into the brake pedal itself: Depress it slowly for inching, fully for braking.

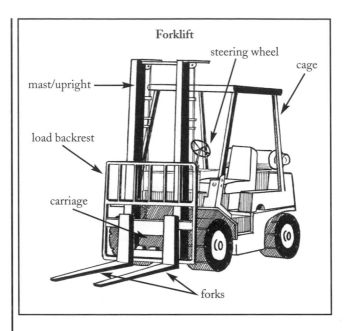

Forklift

steering wheel

cage

mast/upright

load backrest

carriage

forks

Insider Tip

- Mention that you have handled concrete blocks and paper rolls. Add that you have used 2,000- to 10,000-pound units (these refer to the forklift's lifting capacity, not the weight of the unit itself), as well as units equipped with paper-roll clamps. You might also say that you've handled "your fair share" of four-wheel sit-downs, walk-behinds, and pallet trucks.
- Ask about the number of trailers and the number of pallets you will be expected to handle per day (fewer is better).
- Since most people who operate forklifts are not licensed to do so, don't worry that you do not have a license to show.

Brain Surgeon

Brain surgeons train for as long as eight years after medical school, so you should be, or appear to be, at least 34.

Attire
Wear:
- Suit and tie

  or
- Blouse and skirt

Do Not Wear:
- White lab coat or scrubs
- Stethoscope around your neck

Paraphernalia to Bring
- Surgical loupe. Loupes are worn like glasses or over glasses and provide strong magnification during surgery. They are custom-fitted and all brain surgeons have them. Borrow a pair, or carry an empty loupe case. The case should be wooden with a surgeon's name engraved on a metal template. Keep the name on the template obscured. If you cannot borrow an actual loupe or case, substitute a wood case about 10 inches long by 5 inches wide. Do not wear surgical loupes on a chain around your neck, as you would reading glasses or sunglasses.
- Do not carry other surgical instruments.
- Do not carry medical charts.

how to get a job you're not qualified for

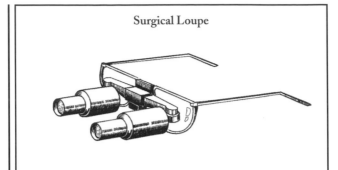

Surgical Loupe

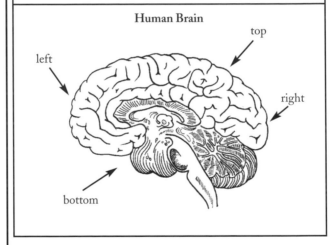

Human Brain

top

left

right

bottom

Buzzwords to Use
- Surgical drill (for drilling into bone)
- Deep brain stimulation (abbreviated DBS, targets particular areas of the brain with electrical pulses)
- Spinal instrumentation (implantation of permanent therapeutic devices in the spine)

CRITICAL KNOWLEDGE
- Ask about the hospital's type of operating microscope and its image-guidance system. Also ask about the strength of the magnet in the hospital's MRI (magnetic resonance imager).
- All brain surgery begins with either drilling or sawing through the cranium.

INSIDER TIP
- Interviewers will want to know about papers you have published in well-known medical journals. Mention that you are awaiting publication in *Neurosurgery* (frequently called the "red journal"), the *Journal of Neurosurgery* (known as the "white journal"), and are expecting a book contract.

SHOE SALESPERSON

Shoe sales has become a much less service-oriented business in recent years, so involved and caring salespeople are hard to find. Make sure you appear to be friendly with a ready smile and that you are well dressed.

ATTIRE
Wear:
- Conservative suit and tie
  or
- Tasteful blouse and skirt
- Socks
- Clean, shined shoes, without scuffs

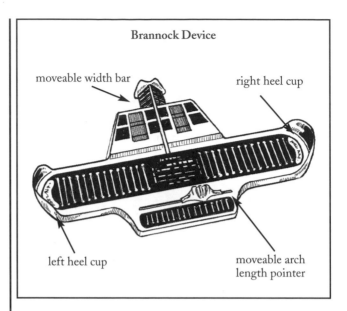

Brannock Device

moveable width bar

right heel cup

left heel cup

moveable arch
length pointer

Do Not Wear:
- Sneakers
- Flip-flops
- Heavy cologne or perfume

Buzzwords to Use
- Brannock Device (the metal foot measurer)
- Slippage (either toe or heel)
- Trees (short for "shoe trees")

Critical Knowledge
- A good fit should leave ¼-inch of room between the big toe and the tip of the shoe. There should be no slippage.

- Shoes with four or five eyelets will take a 36-inch lace, while athletic shoes will generally take a 40- to 45-inch lace.

Insider Tip
- If the patron needs a half-size larger but it is not available, substitute a "wide" style of the lower full size (i.e., a 7 wide for a 7½).
- Shoes that will be worn on a daily basis should be fitted at the end of the day, when the feet have expanded.
- "Toe length" refers to the total length of the foot.

HOW TO SURVIVE
THE INTERVIEW

IF YOU ARE LATE

1 Call ahead.
If you are stuck in traffic or otherwise running late, call as soon as you know you will be substantially late. Ask to reschedule, either later in the day or on another day.

2 Clean yourself up.
Use a bathroom before meeting your interviewer if you are sweaty and disheveled when you arrive. Wash your face with cold water and blot it dry with paper towels. Gargle. Check your teeth for pieces of food.

3 Apologize.
Tell the interviewer you are sorry for your tardiness, but do not overdo the apology. Do not fabricate an explanation that can easily be verified. The following are acceptable excuses, if true.
• The traffic was terrible.
• There was an accident on the bridge.
• My car caught on fire.
• I was stuck in the elevator.
• I had to take my mother/daughter/pet to the emergency room.

Do not say:

- My alarm clock is broken.
- I lost track of the time.
- I couldn't find my belt.
- I was out so late last night . . .

If You Are Asked a Difficult or Leading Question

⭐ Always respond with a positive.
If the interviewer says, "I see you don't have experience," counter with, "That's true, but I've always wanted to learn and I'm a quick study!"

⭐ Use personal experiences to demonstrate strengths in areas that are professionally weak.
If the interviewer asks about project management experience and you don't have any, talk about planning your wedding or organizing a large family function (hiring vendors, designing a database, and creating seating charts based on the interests of guests).

⭐ Answer confidently.
It isn't always what you say, but how you say it. Often, questions are designed to assess your professional attitude and maturity level more than your knowledge base. Be sincere in your responses, and act professionally—even if you don't have a good answer. Be straightforward, even when your answer is "I don't know."

Memorize the following good answers to these standard hard-to-address questions:

Q: Where do you see yourself in five years?

A: At a good job in this industry, at a good company, learning and contributing to the company's growth.

Q: Why should I hire you?

A: I've got the right experience, I understand your needs, and I'm a good team player—both in the office and on the softball field.

Q: Why did you quit your last job?

A: I simply wasn't able to contribute to the company's future in the way I wanted. I'm looking for more opportunities for myself, and for a company that can fully utilize my abilities.

Prepare a last-resort response.

If you are asked the one question you dreaded, take a page from the politicians' playbook: Acknowledge the question, then move on. Say, "I'm very glad you asked that, and I'd like to give it some thought. But I'd really like to discuss . . ."

Be Aware

- Always remember the three C's: Cool, Calm, and Confident. An interview is as much about you wanting the job as it is about the job wanting you.

- Always remember the three A's: Ask a lot of questions, Appear clean-cut and well-dressed, and Act to impress.

- Avoid scheduling interviews just after lunch, when most people get sleepy and irritable.

How to Know If You Are Tanking

1 Watch the interviewer's eyes.
An interviewer that is simply going through the motions will not make eye contact. Check for a glazed or glassy stare and heavy or droopy eyelids.

2 Listen carefully.
A bored or disinterested interviewer may quietly hum a tune, whistle softly, or shuffle papers repeatedly.

3 Observe the interviewer's actions.
An interviewer who is constantly checking the time, eating a sandwich, or takes lots of phone calls probably won't offer you the job.

staring at computer   talking on phone

eating sandwich

Watch for signs of a disinterested interviewer.

4 Pay attention to the amount of time your interviewer speaks versus the amount of time you speak.

If your interviewer speaks more than you do, you may not be coming across very strongly. (On the other hand, some less-experienced interviewers love to hear themselves talk, and may come away with the impression that the interview was very interesting.)

5 Attempt to rescue the situation.

Your goal at this point should simply be to make it through this interview to the next phase of interviewing, where you can hopefully make a stronger impression. Pick one or more of the following statements designed to get you back in front of the interviewer for a second shot:

- "I'm so certain I'm the right person for this job, I'd be willing to bet my first month's paycheck I'll be your top candidate after round two."
- "The insider knowledge I gained at [*insert name of major competitor here*] definitely gives me an edge over any other prospective hire. I look forward to talking again soon."
- "The work I did for the CIA/FBI/NSA makes me the perfect choice for this position. I'd love to tell you more about it at a second interview, provided that you have the necessary clearance."

Be Aware

No matter how well the rest of the interview seems to go, you may not be offered the job if any of the following mishaps occur:

- You ask if a photo on your interviewer's desk is his daughter, and it turns out to be his wife.
- You ask to go to the bathroom three times or more, or one trip lasts more than 15 minutes.
- You don't take off your headset during the interview.
- You receive and respond to more than two cell phone calls.
- You make a cell phone call.
- You answer, "A beer would be nice," when your interviewer asks if you'd like something to drink.

how to survive the interview

HOW TO DISGUISE
A TATTOO

1 Wear long sleeves.
Long-sleeve shirts can cover arm and shoulder tattoos. The garment should be a dark, medium-weight
fabric, not sheer or ultrathin; light-weight white
shirts and blouses will not effectively cover upper-
body tattoos in bright light.

2 Wear a scarf and hat.
A tasteful scarf (for women) or ascot (for men) can be
used to hide neck tattoos. A wide-brimmed hat is
effective for concealing forehead tattoos.

3 Wear boots.
Cover ankle tattoos with ankle boots, but they should
be worn to an interview only if accompanied by a
pantsuit or a long skirt. Do not wear cowboy boots or
high-top lace-up shoes to a job interview.

4 Wear pants or dark stockings.
For leg tattoos, wear pants, or use cosmetics (see step
5) and wear black or off-black medium sheer hosiery;
ultra-sheer hosiery will not hide a tattoo. (Colored
tattoos may be noticeable even through opaque stockings without the preliminary application of makeup.)

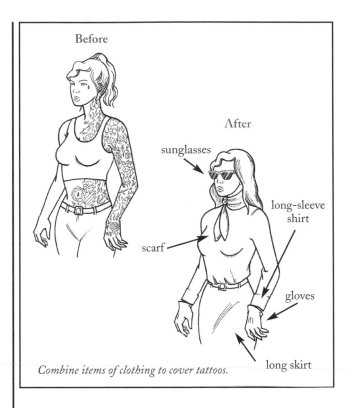

Before

After

sunglasses

long-sleeve
shirt

scarf

gloves

long skirt

Combine items of clothing to cover tattoos.

5 Apply a layer of eye shadow over the tattoo.
Use matte shadow without sparkle. Depending on the
tattoo's colors and complexity, you may need to apply
multiple colors of eye shadow:

- Dark tattoo colors (black, blue, purple): Use yellow
  eye shadow to cover.
- Red: Use light green eye shadow to cover.
- Yellow: Use light to medium pink eye shadow
  to cover.

how to disguise a tattoo

If no eye shadow is available, use colored makeup. Apply green foundation to red shades in a tattoo, pink to yellow shades, and yellow concealer (usually used to cover dark circles under the eyes) for black, blue, or purple in the tattoo.

6 Apply full-coverage makeup.
Use a layer of thick, full-coverage foundation that matches your skin tone. Cover with a dusting of translucent powder to set the coverage. Allow the makeup to dry.

How to Disguise a Piercing

1 Fill holes evenly with wax filler.
Wax filler is available at most department stores. Use slightly softened beeswax if no filler is available.

2 Touch up the area with a full-coverage makeup.
Use a base that matches your skin tone.

3 Dust with translucent powder.
Use a fluffy cosmetic brush.

4 Remove excess powder or makeup.
Use an ear swab.

5 Wear glasses with thick frames.
The glasses can be either corrective or clear. The frames will obscure an eyebrow piercing and distract from a nose or lip piercing.

6 | Shade a lip piercing with a lip pencil.
Choose a lip pencil that matches your natural lip color or wear a colored lipstick. Matte-finish lip pencils with long-lasting color stay are most effective; avoid soft lip pencils. Avoid wearing lipgloss or ultra-shiny lipsticks—the extra shine will draw more attention to your lips.

Be Aware
- Multiple ear piercings can be concealed with hair; use hairspray to keep the hair in place.
- In a pinch, wear bandages to conceal tattoos, but never on the face.

How to Fake a Tattoo or Piercing

 Wear or draw temporary tattoos.
Draw with an indelible marker or apply a temporary tattoo to your forearm, neck, hands, or shoulders several hours before the interview and allow it to dry completely. Pick a tattoo that matches the job.
- Yin/yang—health store clerks, coffeeshop workers
- Mermaids—dockworkers, fishermen
- Blood, thorns—bike messengers
- "Mother"—bouncers, mechanics

Wear clip-on earrings or magnetic nose rings.
An ear cuff may also be used in the nose to simulate a nose piercing.

Trace the appropriate fake tattoo design on your body.

★ Do not play with the fake rings or stare at the "tattoos."
Treat the piercings or tattoos as if they have always been a part of your body.

★ Do not perspire.
Even though most temporary tattoos claim to be long-lasting and sweat resistant, perspiration can cause the tattoo to stain clothing or furniture, and fake piercings can become slippery and slide off.

Be Aware

Do not expose tattoos and jewelry completely. Place your fake tattoos just above a pants line, or below a sleeve. Hide piercings behind strands of hair, allowing you to naturally brush it back at some point to reveal the "piercing." A little exposure can be more natural and convincing than a fully visible tattoo.

CHAPTER 2
PEOPLE SKILLS

HOW TO DEAL WITH A NIGHTMARE BOSS

THE CONTROL FREAK

The Control Freak will attempt to micromanage your every task and responsibility.

⭐ Bombard him with information.
Copy him on every e-mail even remotely involving him or his area of responsibility. Leave towering stacks of reports and copies of all correspondence on his desk. Include him in the most mundane meetings and discussions. You may be able to short-circuit his control mechanism with the sheer volume of data.

⭐ Solicit his opinion, but control the options.
If you must leave a decision up to your boss, offer the solution you favor and two or three lame options—ridiculous or unworkable possibilities that will direct him to choose your course of action. Using phrases such as "You've probably already thought of this" and "I tried to put myself in your shoes when I worked on this" will help you gain favor.

⭐ Remain calm and pleasant.
When your boss interferes with your work or second-guesses your decision, do not become defensive or combative. Say, "How ridiculous—I should have thought of that. Thank goodness I included you!" and

then lead your boss back to your position, while encouraging him to think you're following his guidance.

★ Continue to do your job.
Bide your time. Your boss may ultimately believe that he's shown you the way and he can now go on to help others.

The Buddy

The Buddy will generally attempt to blur the lines between employee and supervisor, soliciting personal information and seeking inclusion as though you are the best of friends. Include the Buddy in small ways, but keep your distance.

★ Invent a hobby.
Avoid sharing intimate details of your real life by inventing a hobby, which you can discuss with her in minute detail. Your fictional toothpick sculptures or love of steam locomotives will become of great interest to the Buddy and can serve as the basis of your "friendship." Movies, restaurants, and sports are also safe, impersonal topics to raise.

★ Offer social invitations you know she can't accept.
Invite her to lunch on a day you are certain she has another appointment. Ask her out for a drink with "the gang" after work on the night she always goes to her yoga class, or when she will be away on business.

Be aware that she may proffer invitations in return, which easily can be evaded by inventing a nightly class of your own.

★ Avoid hugs.
If she attempts to throw a friendly arm around you, fake a sneeze. Blame allergies rather than perfume, which she can change. Your "allergies" can then also become a topic of friendly conversation.

The Workaholic

The Workaholic has lost all sense of perspective, and has sacrificed his life to his job. He will expect the same of you.

★ Present evidence of the real world.
Replace all calendars he sees with ones depicting tropical retreats, ski slopes, or other vacation locales. Litter the office with travel brochures, and purchase office subscriptions to food, travel, and entertainment magazines. E-mail him regularly with weather updates of distant cities.

★ Discuss family at every opportunity.
Show him pictures of your family. Show him pictures of his own family. If even your most distant relative has bought a car, won a part in a school play, or suffered a toothache, offer these stories in careful detail—perhaps they will trigger recognition that he, too, has a wife, sister, uncle, or son.

★ If he has ever discussed a personal interest, become obsessed with it.
Pounce on any non-work-related subject in the hope of rekindling his own passion. Discuss popular subjects and pastimes to spark some vestigial interest. Try baseball, politics, food, music, and celebrity gossip. Avoid even juicy office gossip, since that will lead him back to work-related issues.

THE TELLER OF BAD JOKES

His jokes are always bad.

★ Be prepared.
Steel yourself for the punchline. If you are unable to determine if the punchline has been delivered, watch your boss for response cues such as a long pause or an expectant grin.

★ Determine the nature of the required reaction.
A secure boss will be satisfied with a friendly groan and head shaking, while an insecure boss will require a more elaborate show of amusement and appreciation. Respond accordingly.

★ Fake amusement.
THE SHOULDER SHAKE—Smile, cover your mouth with one hand, and shake your shoulders up and down. This is especially good for puns.
THE AMUSED CHUCKLE—Smile, look directly at your boss, and say, "Heh, heh, heh." This is a versatile, all-purpose laugh response.

The Genuine Guffaw—Smile broadly, then let out a single, loud "Ha!" Slap your thigh in amusement. If seated, slap your knee.

 Change the subject immediately.
Do not give him the chance to "tell you another one."

Be Aware
Be on guard for other styles of bad boss behavior, and be prepared to take quick action:

- The Supreme Delegator
  Always willing to accept all of the credit but none of the blame, the Supreme Delegator is really setting up others to take the fall. Although she tries to cloak her behavior in an air of confidence, the Supreme Delegator has very low self-esteem and fears that she will fail.

  From the moment a project is handed off to you, through all the key decisions, to the final action, make sure you advise your boss—in writing—of all key decisions and plans. Keep copies. Do not be afraid to proceed as you think best, but be prepared for your boss to disavow all knowledge of the details should there be a problem.

- The Yes/No Manager
  This boss is ever-increasingly bored with meaningful information, intelligent discussion, and any complexity. He wants every decision reduced to an overly simplified YES or NO.

  Present an executive summary, with several alternatives for action. Attach the full report with well-reasoned, well-documented arguments for each point. If asked for your recommendation, give it orally.

- **THE PASSIVE-AGGRESSIVE BOSS**
The Passive-Aggressive Boss puts things off, then complains at the last minute that he has not had enough time. The boss can then blame those above or below him for doing a bad job.

Be firm with deadlines and set them in writing. Involve others in the process when possible. These co-workers can then serve as witnesses to any misbehavior on your boss's part.

- **THE INDECISION MAKER**
This boss ascended to power by a fluke—he can't actually make a decision himself. He needs input from three or four different sources in order to feel comfortable in his own shoes.

Present any question to your boss as if you've taken an informal survey. Include information from any key employees he'd want to hear from.

- **THE ALL-BUSINESS-IS-PERSONAL MANAGER**
The All-Business-Is-Personal Manager has a seriously dysfunctional life outside of work, and thus cannot ever really separate business life from personal life. He will take everything personally. He has nothing but work to cling to, so make your work time with him enjoyable. One bad day can ruin a whole relationship.

HOW TO DEAL WITH A NIGHTMARE CO-WORKER

THE TALKER

The Talker just won't shut up.

⭐ Look busy.
Free time means chat time to the Talker. Leave paperwork handy on your desk, and spreadsheets or other documents open on your computer at all times. When the Talker approaches, stare at the task intently and pretend not to notice his arrival.

⭐ Evade and deflect.
Say, "I'd love to hear more, but I've got to finish this by [fifteen minutes from now]." Or, rise from your desk and say, "Oh my gosh, I've got to go to that meeting." As you walk away, suggest that another co-worker has expressed interest in whatever is on the Talker's mind and aim him in that direction.

⭐ "Yes" the conversation to death.
Talkers are often of the life-is-a-struggle type, for whom everything is a hardship, and they must convince you of this. As the Talker's tale unfolds, keep agreeing with the Talker, but be sure you do not ask a question or volunteer information. After five flat

agreements ("Yes . . . yes, I see.") the Talker should count this as adequate confirmation and wander off.

⭐ Avoid showing emotion.
Do not be cheerful around the Talker, as this may make her dejected and even more talkative. Do not be sad around the Talker, since this may encourage him to top your tale of woe with his own.

The Kiss-Up

The Kiss-Up craves approval mostly from the boss, but will also seek approval from you.

⭐ Congratulate her on her dedication and achievements, no matter how dubious:
"You've sure got a way with a spreadsheet," "It's not everyone who'd work five straight weekends," or "You make the *best* coffee."

⭐ Get her to do some of your own work as well.
Suggest that this is a good way to further bring her talents to the boss's attention.

⭐ Avoid her during restructuring.
During times of management turmoil or when the chain of command is uncertain, the Kiss-Up may become disoriented or hostile. Give her a wide berth.

The TMI (Too Much Information)

TMIs have no boundaries and no shame. Every unsettling piece of personal information is worth sharing with you.

★ Avoid TMIs on Mondays.
The weekend will provide him with an abundance of ammunition for inappropriate personal tales. By Tuesday or Wednesday, he may have expended the most harrowing of these stories on fellow workers.

★ Do not get on an elevator with a TMI.
If you see a TMI waiting for an elevator, take the stairs. If you are already inside the elevator, feign some activity—a forgotten wallet, pocketbook, or keys—that will provide an excuse for your quickly exiting to retrieve the item.

★ Maintain a buffer of at least two co-workers between the TMI and yourself at any company party or off-site function.
If the first co-worker bolts, you will still have time for evasive maneuvers as the TMI engages the second.

★ Say, "Thanks for sharing."
Upon the completion of a long and sordid tale—his tapeworm, his night on the town, or his dream about the boss—say "Thanks for sharing." Without further comment or response from you, the TMI will move on to seek a more appreciative audience.

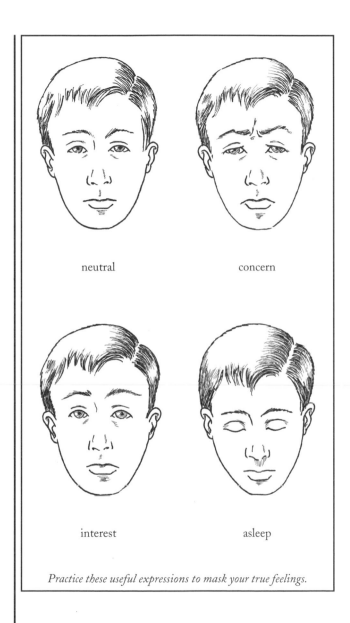

neutral

concern

interest

asleep

Practice these useful expressions to mask your true feelings.

how to deal with a nightmare co-worker

The Gossip

While sharing many of the characteristics of the TMI, the Gossip specializes in spreading too much information about other people.

 Beware the signs.

A sure sign of a hopeless (but amateur) gossip is someone who proceeds a statement with, "I shouldn't be telling you this but . . ." or, "I promised I wouldn't tell anyone but . . ." Apply the techniques for avoiding a TMI, above, to save yourself from a gossip who wants to tell you everything.

 Bait and switch.

Offer outrageous stories about yourself in order to stun and distract him from prying into your true private life. With a serious expression, tell the Gossip that you were locked in the monkey cage at the zoo all weekend and had the time of your life; or that you accidentally sent a very revealing personal photo via e-mail to all the executives in the company. The juicier the story, the better. When he asks, "Is that true?" say, "I'm sorry, I can't talk about it anymore."

HOW TO DEAL WITH A NIGHTMARE CUSTOMER

IRATE RETAIL CUSTOMER

1 Watch for warning signs.
A customer will usually display several "build up" physical cues before becoming irate. Look for clenching of the hands, locking of the knees, crossing of the arms, rolling of the eyes, and leaning in toward you to reduce the amount of personal space between you.

2 Listen, listen, listen.
The customer will raise his voice and become demanding, and may begin assessing blame, claiming victimhood, threatening to report you, and insisting on satisfaction. Let him rant—interrupting or defending your actions during the rant will only exacerbate the problem.

3 Do not mimic the posture or volume of the irate patron.
Avoid leaning in, but do not lean away, either: Moving away indicates that you are becoming defensive. Maintain a placid, neutral position.

Remain calm.

4 Stay loose.

Keep your weight evenly distributed on both feet. Breathe deeply and exhale slowly.

5 Speak softly.

Wait until the customer is finished speaking, then speak calmly. Never state that the customer is angry or upset. Instead, say, "I recognize that you are raising your voice. What is it you need me to do? What is it you need the store to do?" Anger results from unmet needs, so try your best to solve the problem.

6 Send a clear message and offer a clear resolution.
Say, "My commitment is to a quick, successful resolution of this problem." Offer an exchange, a return, or a new item according to your company's policies. If you are unable to provide a satisfactory solution, ask a manager for help.

7 Apologize.
Before you find a manager, say, "I am sorry we were unable to help you today. I do hope that you will come back to shop at our store again."

ABUSIVE RESTAURANT PATRON

1 Listen.
Allow the customer to explain what is wrong. If he begins yelling or using foul language, do not respond in kind.

2 Do not argue.
If the customer complains that the food is a funny color, that the bread is stale, or that the coffee tastes of detergent, do not respond by saying, "It looks/tastes okay to me!" Never taste a customer's food.

3 Observe the customer.
If the customer stands up angrily, moves in close, or begins gesticulating wildly, move away and quietly ask him to lower his voice. If he refuses, or if he starts poking or grabbing the food, ask him to leave.

4 Observe the room.

Quickly check the room to see if other diners are being disturbed. If you notice turned heads or whispering, contact the manager immediately to deal with the other customers, or to back you up with yours.

5 Placate.

Keep your tone even and your volume low. If a dish is unsatisfactory, offer to take it back and provide him with another selection. If the customer's dinner arrived late or cold, offer to remove it from the bill.

6 Check back.

Once the problem is resolved, check back with the customer to make certain everything is acceptable. Do not check more than once. Consider offering a dessert or after-dinner drink "on the house."

Be Aware

- Watch for a setup. A customer may eat and complain in hopes of getting a complimentary meal. If a customer returns to the restaurant to dine and complains again, alert the manager and consider asking the patron to leave and not return.

- Avoid physical confrontation with patrons, particularly if the tables in the restaurant are close together.

HOW TO
SURVIVE THE
OFFICE PICNIC

1 Do not enter the picnic alone.
If you arrive early, wait until you see a group enter, then tag along with the crowd. This reduces the possibility of being forced into conversation with the one or two people already there.

2 Lay the groundwork for an early departure.
Upon arrival, tell your boss a convincing story that would necessitate leaving early. Mention that the sitter has another obligation, that your dog is sick at home alone (whether you have a dog or not), that you have the beginnings of the flu, or another appropriate excuse. Apologize and act sorry that you will not be able to stay longer. Should you decide to escape quickly, your early exit will not seem abrupt.

3 Control your alcohol intake.
You risk embarrassment (or worse) if you get drunk in front of your colleagues. Have no more than one drink at the beginning of the picnic to help you relax, then limit your consumption to one drink per hour. Make sure you eat, too.

Food is a safe topic for company picnic conversation.

4 Talk about the food.

If you find yourself stuck with people you don't know (or don't like), discuss the food. It is a common topic for picnic conversation and may lead to discussion of restaurants, travel, and other easy subjects. Other safe topics include the weather, the latest celebrity divorce, television programs, sports, movies, and books. Avoid talking about the physical attractiveness of other employees, the incompetence of managers, the annoying habits of your co-workers, or diseases of any kind.

5 Avoid discussing work.
It's best to avoid all topics relating to the company itself, including projects, policies, culture, and co-workers. Alcohol can loosen tongues, and you may not know everyone within earshot, nor their allegiances. Assume that everything you say will be repeated, out of context, to the person you don't want to hear it.

6 Do not be the first to leave.
Unless you prepared upon your arrival for an early departure (see step 2), do not be the first person to leave. Wait for two or three other people to go, and depart shortly thereafter. If you observe your boss checking the time as people are leaving, delay your exit for another 15 to 20 minutes.

IF YOU BECOME INTOXICATED

1 Do not talk to your boss.
Excuse yourself from any conversations with bosses, managers, or co-workers who might later recount any of your inappropriate comments or behavior.

2 If you become trapped in a conversation with your boss, become a "Yes man."
Smile, nod, and find a way out.

3 Spill something.
As a last resort, knock your drink over on the table, or spill it on yourself. Then excuse yourself to go wash up. The person or persons you were talking to will move on to another conversation.

4 Withdraw.

Find an out-of-the-way tree or park bench. Ask for help from a colleague if you cannot make it on your own, but get out of harm's way before you damage your reputation.

5 Do not return.

Take a walk and drink plenty of water. If you cannot sober up, have a colleague tell your boss that you had to leave "because something suddenly came up."

HOW TO MAKE AN IMPROMPTU TOAST

1 Keep it simple.
A toast made in front of colleagues should be brief and safe.

2 Follow the "Past, Present, Future" (PPF) rule.
Acknowledge past successes, present situations, and future objectives. For example: "We've been through a difficult year together, but in the end, we made it a successful one. I can think of no better team to be moving forward with—I love working with all of you. Here's to a bright and successful future together."

3 Avoid problems.
Stay away from losses, morale problems, indictments, former employees, or other natural or human-made disasters. If the last year has been truly horrible, refer to it in a neutral, ambiguous way: "It's been quite a year . . ." or, "As this extraordinary year comes to an end . . ." If the problems are continuing and you don't want to lie, say something emphatic but meaningless: "What a group of people to work with!" or, "I've never worked with a group like this!" or, "The talents and abilities of all of you continue to amaze me!" The future is the easiest portion of the toast, since you can hope and wish without regard to reality. Nonetheless, moderation is best: "The coming year promises to be astonishing!" or, "The sky's the limit in the year ahead."

Be brief. No one is really listening.

4 Focus on the people.

Your toast should be about people in general—about spirit, creativity, and bonding—rather than about specific financial results, projects undertaken, or company goals. All of the partygoers are hoping you don't mention them by name, and they really want to get back to eating and drinking.

5 Use humor judiciously.

A little levity may be appreciated, but jokes can slow down your toast and breed restlessness. Depending upon your condition, you may be in no position to gauge what is funny. Attempts at humor could backfire and insult people, open wounds, or just be incomprehensible. If a remark or a joke bombs, keep going. Pausing will only call attention to it and add to the audience's discomfort.

6 Smile, nod, and look proud as you are speaking.

Keep your glass raised and lift it even higher as you conclude the toast. Remember, no one is really listening, anyway.

HOW TO SURVIVE A WORKPLACE ROMANCE

★ Do not tell colleagues.
Do not discuss any aspect of your relationship with anyone at work, even close friends. Avoid telltale references, such as, "When we were at the movies last night . . . " Do not play guessing games with co-workers, such as, "I'm going out with someone from the office but you'll never guess who."

★ Resist physical contact at the office.
Avoid all physical contact, including kissing, hand-holding, hugging, casual touching, and back rubs, even if you think you are alone. Maintain at least a foot of personal space between you and the person you are dating.

★ Send gifts to the home.
Do not have flowers, candy, clothing, or other personal items sent to the office, even with an unsigned card: People will begin asking questions.

★ Do not use company e-mail to send personal notes.
Many employers monitor e-mail messages, and even deleted messages are stored. It is also too easy to send an e-mail to the wrong person or to "everyone."

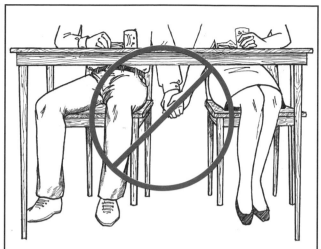

Avoid physical contact in the office, even when you think no one else is looking.

★ Avoid long or excessive lunch dates.
While it is accceptable for colleagues to eat together, extended or repeated outings may attract notice. Maintain the lunch routine you practiced before you started dating your co-worker.

★ Avoid arriving and departing together.
Unless you are in a car pool with others, stagger your arrival and departure times.

★ Use discretion.
At company picnics or parties, or at off-site meetings, do not drink excessively, dance intimately, or openly display affection with your office significant other.

Be Aware
- Most office romances begin in the spring.
- Dating more than one person from the same company at the same time is not a good idea.

The Break-Up

Do not break up at work.

Emotions can be difficult to hide, and people can act irrationally when they are upset. The workplace, especially in a cubicle but even in a private office, is a poor choice of location for a confrontation. Avoid breaking up over lunchhour, as well.

Break up over a long weekend.

Choose a time when your partner will have several days to heal before having to see you at the office. Try to be sensitive to his or her feelings, however: Do not break up just before the other person leaves on an extended vacation.

Be prepared for the worst.

A bad break-up may require you to transfer or even resign, particularly if you are dating someone above you in the office hierarchy. Ending a relationship with someone who reports to you could lead to a charge of sexual discrimination.

⭐ Do not immediately begin dating someone else at work.

Your new relationship may be hurtful to your ex, if you are spotted. You may also gain a reputation for being opportunistic or desperate.

⭐ Do not discuss personal feelings or emotions with your ex while at work.

If you want to check on how your former lover is doing, call at home.

Be Aware

No matter what you call it—fishing off the company pier, mentoring the intern, kissing company cousins, refilling the toner, mergers and acquisitions—office romances are dangerous.

CHAPTER 3

ON-THE-JOB
SURVIVAL

HOW TO SURVIVE IN A TINY WORKSPACE

CUBICLE

1 Select a good location.
Opt for a cube away from main hallways, bathrooms, supply rooms, and other high-traffic areas, if you have the choice. Avoid cubes within the boss's line of sight.

2 Use comfort devices.
Requisition a more comfortable chair, or select one from an empty cubicle or office (some styles of chairs may be assigned to employees above a certain level, so be careful about what you borrow). Alternatively, obtain a doctor's note stating that you require a comfortable chair for medical reasons—your employer will be obligated to provide you with one. A back pillow and footrest will also make cube life more comfortable and relaxed. Do not attempt to fit in recliners, love seats, or hammocks.

3 Install convenience items.
A wireless telephone headset will give you increased freedom of movement. Noise-canceling stereo headphones (with an extra-long cord) will eliminate outside distractions. A small fan is effective in filtering out annoying noises such as typing and phone conversations. (The fan will also make it more difficult for co-workers to eavesdrop on your conver-

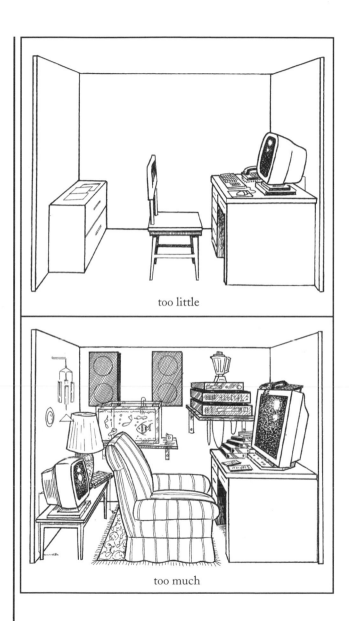

too little

too much

how to survive in a tiny workspace

sations.) Small refrigerators, hair dryers, televisions, VCRs, and blenders should not be easily visible.

4 Personalize your space.
Decorate your cubicle with your family photographs and drawings, as well as other pictures and cartoons you like, giving your cube a homey touch. Avoid hanging too many items or you risk a cubicle that looks like a dorm room or refrigerator door.

5 Build upward.
There is usually no limit to the amount of vertical space you can occupy. Stack in/out trays high atop elevated surfaces for additional room. Staplers, tape dispensers, card files, and other items that traditionally occupy valuable space on top of a desk can be suspended from the ceiling to create a more spacious environment below.

6 Use mirrors.
Hang a large mirror on the cubicle wall to create the illusion of spaciousness.

Be Aware
• Health and safety codes dictate that cubes may not have roofs. Do not attempt to construct a fully-enclosed cubicle for privacy.
• Adding a small, stick-on, wide-angle mirror to the edge of your monitor allows you to see if someone is peering into your cubicle from behind.

- Notify your supervisor that you would like to sit in a "double-wide" cubicle if one becomes available. Standard cubes are 8 by 8 feet and 4 to 6 feet high—double-wides offer twice the floor space of standard units, plus an L- or U-shaped desk. The double-wide cubicle does carry some risk: If office space gets tight, you may find yourself with a cube-mate, a particularly undesirable situation.

HOW TO SURVIVE LIGHT DEPRIVATION DISORDER (LDD)

Working indoors during all of the daylight hours throws off your biological clock. If you work in a building without windows, or if you have a cubicle in the middle of the floor, you are susceptible to LDD.

Increase your exposure to sunlight.
Eat outside at lunchtime. Take your coffee breaks outside. Arrange for meetings outside of the office. Go on regular "market research" field trips. Work in conference rooms with windows.

Use artificial light.
Fill your cubicle with additional desklamps and warm lights (not fluorescents). Install lightboxes that are designed specifically for treating LDD.

Place any lights in front of you.
Arrange lamps or lightboxes so that the light hits the back of your eye. Your goal is to increase the number of photons hitting your retina.

Be Aware

- Symptoms of LDD include insomnia or regular napping, carbohydrate cravings, depression, frustration at normal workday tasks, family problems, loss of libido, emotional disconnect, lethargy, joint pains, stomach problems, lowered resistance to infection, behavioral problems, attitude problems, and alcohol abuse. The disorder is often difficult to detect.
- Even if your workplace has a lot of windows, you are at risk. A corner office with a window is still highly unlikely to get the 2,500 Lux (the level of light the sun emits during daytime hours) your body needs. A well-lit office usually proffers only a few hundred Lux.
- If you work the night shift, avoid light during the day when you are trying to sleep. Blackout curtains and dawn simulation alarm clocks can help you achieve proper conditions.

TRUCK CAB

1 Use a quality seat.
Choose a model (either when ordering the truck or after-market) with heat, massage, and multiple adjustment options. If these are not available, use a portable massager to maintain circulation and a heating blanket for comfort.

2 Install a sunroof.
Natural light from above will make the cab seem more open.

3 Listen to satellite radio and books on CD.
Satellite radio technology offers hundreds of stations, mostly commercial free, that will remain tuned in as you drive. Books will keep you alert and reduce fatigue.

4 Use a hands-free cellular phone with a speaker.
Choose a service with good national coverage and avoid using an ear piece, which can be uncomfortable on long tips.

5 Use a CB or ham radio.
Radios will keep you in contact with other drivers, alert you to traffic tie-ups or accidents, inform you of the location of police, or offer an outlet for conversation.

6 Install a power inverter with two 110-volt receptacles.
These outlets will allow you to easily add items like portable computers, personal digital assistants, and coffee pots. Electronics may also be used for locating freight, sending e-mail, and getting directions.

7 Keep photos nearby.
Pictures will give the cab a more personal feel. If you have children, consider putting some of their drawings on the dashboard.

8 Bring a pet.
Dogs tend to be more amenable to long hauls than cats or fish.

Be Aware

For overnight hauls you can purchase a sleeper cab, which can be personalized to include all the necessities of home, including a toilet, a kitchenette, a television, VCR, DVD player, and cabinets for plenty of storage.

TOLLBOOTH

1 Adjust the seat.

The assigned seat may be hard and uncomfortable. Bring a cushion or a small, folding stadium chair with back support to place on the seat. A massager or vibrating seat pad will also combat discomfort.

2 Adjust interior elements.

Place the chair in an acceptable spot. If the booth has an adjustable table lamp, move it so the light is not in your eyes. Most tollbooths have a computer monitor or an adjustable touch screen on a swivel arm. Position the screen so you can view it comfortably.

3 Install comfort items.

Space heaters provide warmth during cold winter months; fans cool during the hot summer months. A small radio or television will keep your brain active, reducing fatigue. Most highway authorities do not allow "boom boxes."

4 Bring books or games.

Books and crossword puzzles keep your mind occupied in the booth during light traffic periods.

5 Play car-spotting games to help pass the time.
Pick two specific types of cars, and guess which one will pass your booth first. Count the number of cars of a certain color that you see in one day—then try to break your record.

6 Use the intercom.
The booth should have an intercom for communicating with other booths. Chat every now and then, but be aware that supervisors always monitor the channel.

7 Take breaks.
Take advantage of all your rest breaks—at least two 15-minute breaks plus a half hour for lunch. A brisk walk or calisthenics will increase blood flow and make you more alert on the job. Reading—but not watching television—can also be an invigorating break.

8 Drink fluids.
Staying hydrated will keep you sharp and reduce lethargy. Avoid coffee, which dehydrates.

Be Aware
Toll plazas at lightly traveled exits are generally preferable to busy interchanges. Try to arrange for work assignments at less populated areas and avoid the first or last entrance/exit of turnpikes. Time seems to pass more quickly the busier you are, however.

HOW TO SNEAK OUT OF A MEETING

Sneak Out in Plain Sight

1 Establish your presence.
Lay the groundwork for your departure by first making a brief speech, giving a short presentation, or otherwise making your presence known. In this way people will remember that you were there.

2 Call attention to yourself.
Make a show of going out and then coming back into the meeting several times. Say, "Boy, this coffee really goes right through me!" and then go to the restroom twice. Make sure people notice when you return.

3 Make your escape.
The third time you leave, don't return.

Sneak Out Using a Distraction

1 Express interest in attending the meeting.
Before the meeting, say to your boss or a colleague, "I can't wait to see what Phil has to say" or, "Which conference room is the meeting in?" Make it clear that you really want this meeting and, thus, would be the last one to miss it.

2 Sit away from the focus of attention.
Sit on the opposite end of the room from the person running the meeting or from the screen where the presentation will be displayed.

3 Sneak out.
When the lights dim and the presentation begins, quietly get up from your seat. If there are empty chairs around the table, just walk away from your chair. If all the seats are taken, move your chair away from the table against a wall so the vacant chair will not be noticed. Leave the room and don't come back. Have a plausible cover story ready, such as an unexpected visit from a client/customer or a personal emergency regarding your spouse/child/pet.

CRAWL UNDER THE TABLE

1 Assess the size and shape of the table.
The ideal conference table to escape is rectangular and seats at least 12 people, preferably more, with some of the seats left empty. People cluster at the center or at one end of the table if it is not full, usually leaving one or both ends available for an exit route. Do not attempt to sneak away under a round table since you may be surrounded by legs.

2 Slide under the table.
When no one is looking, slide quietly down your chair to the floor. Push your chair against the wall or leave it in its place, depending on how full the table is (see step 3 above). Do not call attention to yourself.

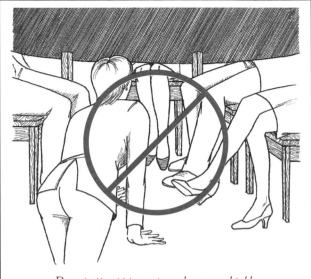

Do not attempt to escape under a round table.

Crawl along the center of the table, avoiding your co-workers' feet.

3 Crawl.
Proceed on your hands and knees under the center of the table. Avoid bumping shins, feet, or loose shoes. If you are discovered, say you are looking for your pen.

4 Monitor conversation.
The end of the table will probably be closest to the door. Wait until someone at a long side of the table is speaking: People will look in that direction.

5 Continue on all fours.
Crawl out from under the table and to the door. Reach up and open the door quietly. Check for people outside.

6 Exit the room.
When the coast is clear, crawl into the hallway.

7 Stand up and walk away.

Be Aware
- If you plan to escape by crawling, wear loose-fitting clothes.
- Most people have limited peripheral vision; when looking straight ahead, they cannot see an object at an angle of more than 45 degrees behind and to the side. Use this as a guide when determining if your escape will be noticed.
- If other escape plans will not work, spill a cup of lukewarm coffee on your pants. This strategy wins sympathy and also offers a perfect excuse for

leaving the meeting. If someone later asks why you never returned, say you got a slight burn. They probably will not seek to verify.

How to Stay Awake During a Meeting

⭐ Use correct meeting posture.
Keep your head up, shoulders back, and spine straight. Keep your legs bent at a 90-degree angle, not fully extended. Feet should be flat on the floor.

⭐ Be on guard for mind-numbing repetition.
Repetitive noise patterns and repetitive images can cause a trance-like state that deadens the senses. If phrases like "need better communication" and "building a team" are repeated, or if tables, graphs, and pie charts are projected endlessly, exit the room for a few minutes.

⭐ Wear sunglasses.
The harsh glare of fluorescent lights can cause eye strain and lead to fatigue. Wear dark glasses.

⭐ Exercise.
Exercise combats fatigue and keeps the mind alert. Take frequent walks around the room or do calisthenics. If possible, jog in place.

⭐ Stay hydrated.
Drink water or sports drinks that provide energy and contain potassium, salt, and carbohydrates. Coffee

contains caffeine, a stimulant that also acts as a diuretic, which will cause dehydration, so drink at least one glass of water for every cup of coffee you consume. This will also promote trips to the bathroom, and consequently, movement and stimulation. Do not drink alcohol: It depresses the nervous system and leads to fatigue.

 Use interrogation techniques.
Pinch yourself, sit in an uncomfortable position, poke your leg with a pen or paper clip, or stare wide-eyed at a bright light—the pain will heighten your awareness.

Be Aware
Warning signs of meeting fatigue include inattentiveness, back tension, shallow breathing, frequent blinking, heavy eyelids, and snoring.

HOW TO COVER YOUR MISTAKES

EXPUNGE A NASTY E-MAIL

⭐ Recall it.
Some e-mail programs allow you to "recall" a message you sent, giving you the option of deleting or replacing it. This feature only works if the recipient is also using the same brand of software and if the recipient is on your local area network. In the Sent Items folder, open the e-mail and click "Recall This Message" on the Tools menu (or Actions menu, depending on which software you have). Follow the instructions.

⭐ Retract it.
Several free software programs or add-ins allow you to "retract" (delete) an e-mail before it is read. Instead of sending the actual message, these programs send the recipient a link to a website that stores your sent e-mail, enabling you to send a "delete" command before the recipient opens the message. If you tend to get angry and impulsive, consider buying such a program.

⭐ Delete the message from the recipient's computer.
As soon as you realize your mistake, call the recipient and send him on a fool's errand, or have the recipient paged to another area. Go to his desk. Kneel so you are not easily visible. Open his e-mail program and

delete the message. Check the "trash" mailbox to make sure it was fully deleted and not just moved. Delete it permanently.

⭐ Claim poor spelling or blame the automatic spell checker.
Insist to the recipient that your message isn't what you meant to say. Explain that the bad language was a typo, or that it was a typo that the automatic spell checker changed into another, unintended word.

⭐ Claim that someone else sent the e-mail from your machine.

⭐ Blame computers generally.
Explain that a moment's frustration was blown way out of proportion because computers make it so easy to vent and send. Claim that before computer technology and e-mail, this never would have happened.

Be Aware

- It is best to queue outgoing e-mail in your outbox rather than send it immediately. This gives you the opportunity to pause and reflect on your wording, and then change or delete the message before it is sent.
- One e-mail program offers a "Mood Watch" function that monitors your typing and alerts you if a message is approaching "flame" status.

SALVAGE A COFFEE-STAINED DOCUMENT

If you are working with a signed contract or a document you cannot replace, you will have to restore the existing pages.

1 Blot the stain immediately.
Use a clean rag or paper towel to remove as much of the coffee as possible before it dries. Blot, do not wipe. The longer the stain sets, the more difficult the removal.

2 Examine the stain.
If the stain caused the ink to run, you are probably dealing with an unsalvageable document. Follow the directions in step 3 to be sure.

3 Determine the printing method.
Wet the end of an ear swab and quickly run it across a non-stained word. If the ink transfers to the cotton, the document was printed on an ink-jet printer and salvage is not possible. Use as is.

4 Make a vinegar solution.
For a small stain (1 to 2 inches in diameter), mix 1 tablespoon white vinegar with 1 tablespoon cold water. (Double or triple the amounts based on stain size.) Pour the mixture into a plate or shallow dish.

5 Place the stained document on the edge of the dish.
Using a metal spoon, weight the stained portion so it rests in the solution. It is not necessary to immerse the entire sheet.

6 Soak for 5 minutes.
If the stain is still present, let the document soak for five additional minutes.

7 Remove from the solution and blot.
Blot the wet area using a clean, dry paper towel. Do not rub.

8 Dry.
For best results, clip the paper to a string with a clothespin or paper clip to expose both sides to the

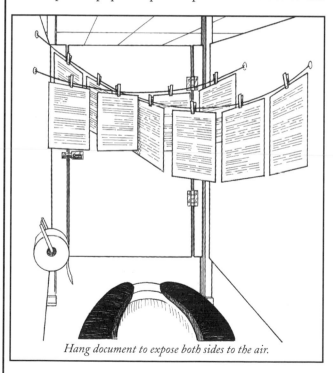

Hang document to expose both sides to the air.

air. Drying time is about 30 minutes. If time is of the essence or the document is very wrinkled, use a warm iron to carefully smooth the stained area and to speed the drying process.

Be Aware

- Do not rub the stained area when the stain is fresh or damp from the vinegar, as you may rip the document.
- Depending on the severity and freshness of the stain, blotting repeatedly with a vinegar-soaked paper towel instead of soaking may be effective for removal. When the stain has faded, blot with a clean, dry paper towel and dry as above.
- If the signature page at the end of a contract is the stained page, do not try to remove the stain. Blot dry and leave alone. The signatories may have used a fountain pen or a type of ink that is water soluble.

Spill on a Patron

1 Apologize immediately.
Even if the spill was clearly the fault of the diner, apologize. The apology must sound sincere.

2 Get club soda and clean napkins.
The carbonation in club soda helps bring the stain to the surface, making for easier cleanup. Use on any stain except red wine or a red wine–based dish like Chateaubriand. If the stain is red wine, go to step 5.

3 Analyze the location of the stain.

Helping in stain removal may not be appropriate, depending on where the stain is located and the sensitivities of the patron. Offer the club soda and napkins to another guest at the table and suggest that the guest assist the diner with stain removal in the restroom. If the stain is on a jacket, offer to take the jacket and work on the stain. (Most stains occur over the right shoulder, since drinks are served and cleared from this side.)

4 Replace the spilled beverage or food item.

5 Offer to pay for dry cleaning.

For a red-wine stain, you or the manager should offer to have the clothing cleaned at the restaurant's expense. You might also offer a complimentary dessert or bottle of wine on the diner's next visit.

Fix a Bad Haircut

If the Cut Is Uneven

1 Offer to make good.

Explain to the customer that you can fix the haircut. Avoid offering a refund. If the client insists, offer several free hair-care products instead.

2 Keep cutting.

Unless you plan to offer the customer extensions or a hair weave, going shorter is the only way to even out the hair. Make sure you tell the client what you are doing. Say, "I'm taking a little more off the top here, just to even it out." Stop every few minutes and hold up a hand mirror to display the new length.

3 Maintain a sense of humor.

Say, "Didn't I tell you I specialize in asymmetrical haircuts?" If the client is still angry, try compliments: "You know, your hair looks great at this length. We should have cut it shorter a long time ago." Avoid getting defensive.

4 Use camouflage.

Hide the uneven cut by slicking back all the hair with a heavy, wet-look gel. The glare of the gel under lights or sunlight may make the short side difficult to see.

5 Use the ears.

An uneven section of hair can often be hidden behind one ear. Apply gel to slick the hair back and behind the ear, and a good dusting of hairspray to hold it in place.

6 Accessorize.

Place a large hair clip on the shorter side to obscure your mistake. If the accessory will not cover the short section, put it on the longer side to attract the eye and draw attention away from the shorter side.

Before

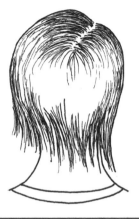

After

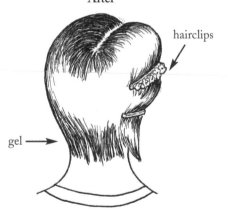

hairclips

gel

To hide an uneven cut, apply a heavy, wet-look gel. Hair clips distract attention.

★ **Re-dye.**
Using the ten-level system to classify hair color (1 is black, 3 is darkest brown, 5 is medium brown, 7 is dark blond, and 10 is very light blond, with all other colors falling somewhere in between), make sure the new dye color is no more than two levels above the natural hair color. If the natural color cannot be discerned, use the existing color as your baseline.

★ **Go brighter, not lighter.**
Dye dark hair a bright color such as auburn, mahogany, or caramel. Any hair color above level 5 should never be given blond highlights.

★ **Apply a color glaze.**
If the highlights are too light (too much bleach), use a conditioning color glaze to tone down the highlights, then re-highlight with a hair color. Avoid using more bleach at all costs.

★ **Go dark.**
Light-colored hair—or any hair—easily can be made darker. Do not change the color by more than two levels (see step 1). If the hair has a damaged, orange hue, use a color with an ash tint to cut the orange.

Be Aware

Many home coloring treatments are bad for the hair shaft and can damage follicles and cause hair to fall out. If you run out of professional hair color, make a healthy substitute. For dark color, mix already brewed, damp coffee grounds with regular shampoo until the mix is the color you are seeking. Wash the hair normally and rinse well for a quick-and-dirty (but safe) dye job. To lighten hair, mix hair gel with standard iodine.

HOW TO SURVIVE IF YOU ARE CAUGHT SLACKING

SURFING THE WEB

⭐ Blame your search engine.
Explain that your search engine mistakenly has provided you with an address to an inappropriate site. Alternatively, claim you made a typing error in the Web address.

⭐ Blame your browser.
Say that someone has set a new "home page" on your Internet browser. Sounding annoyed, loudly ask, "Who keeps setting my browser to open on this sports page? I'm trying to get those new numbers for my report!" You can also claim that you're having trouble loading certain work-related websites and so you are visiting more popular sites to see if the computer is working properly.

⭐ Blame the website.
Claim that the window with inappropriate material opened unexpectedly while you were viewing something else. Lament that such "pop-ups" are very common and should be regulated.

Blame an e-mail correspondent.
Claim that someone sent you the hyperlink, and you clicked it without knowing what it was.

Be Aware
- When surfing the Web, always keep the corporate intranet site up in a separate browser window. Be ready to click over quickly.
- Position your monitor at an angle that prevents anyone standing at the entrance to your office or cube from viewing the screen.

ASLEEP AT YOUR DESK

 Blame work.
Say, "I'm so exhausted; I was here until midnight last night!" Do not attempt this if your boss works late and you do not.

 Blame medication.
Claim that your new allergy medicine has been making you drowsy. Say, "Those antihistamines just knock me out!"

 Blame lunch.
Say, "Wow, I guess I should not have eaten that turkey sandwich. Triptophan really makes me sleepy!"

how to survive if you are caught slacking

The Proper Napping Position

forehead on fingertips

thumb supporting jaw

arm perpendicular to desk

Be Aware

When taking a nap, always rest your elbow on your desk and keep your arm perpendicular to the desktop. Your forehead should rest on your four fingers—your thumb, spread apart from the fingers, should support your jaw. This position will keep your head up and aimed at your desk. Face in a direction so that it is not immediately visible to someone approaching your desk that your eyes are closed. Keep an important group of documents in your perceived line of sight so as to appear to be reading intently.

HOW TO SURVIVE A NIGHTMARE BUSINESS TRIP

Flying in Coach

1 Be prepared.
Take supplies with you to make the flight more pleasant:
- Good food. Coach-class meals have never been stellar, and you're guaranteed a good meal if you bring something good onboard. Plus, you can eat whenever you wish.
- Neck pillow. The inflatable pillow makes sleeping and even sitting much more comfortable.
- Water. Avoid becoming dehydrated by the plane's air conditioning system.
- Lip balm. Avoid uncomfortable and unsightly chapped lips.

2 Get a seat with extra legroom.
The bulkheads and exit rows usually offer the most room to stretch out. A middle seat in an exit row may be more comfortable than an aisle seat in a non-exit row. Make sure, however, that the seatbacks recline—certain exit rows have non-reclining chairs.

3 Request a seat at the rear of the plane, in a row with open seats.

The rear is not only the safest area in the event of a crash, but it will allow you to board immediately after the first-class passengers, giving you the first available access to the overhead storage bins as well as pillows and blankets. Open seats will allow you to stretch out. Choose a window seat. If you sit on the aisle, you risk being disturbed every time someone in your row wants to get up or every time a person passes on the way to the lavatory. With a window seat, you'll be in control of the shade and have a wall to lean against.

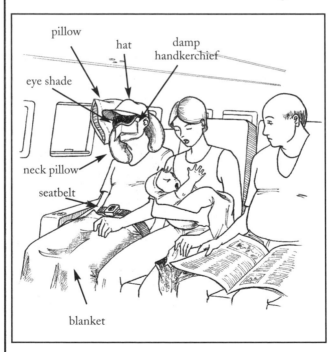

pillow

hat

damp handkerchief

eye shade

neck pillow

seatbelt

blanket

4 Place your carry-on bag in the overhead compartment.
Keep the space under the seat in front of you clear, so you can stretch. If there is no room in the overhead compartment for your bag, place it under another open seat on your row. If you must stash it beneath the seat in front of you, plan to use it as a footrest by pulling it out slightly.

5 Make yourself comfortable.
Remove your shoes, as feet tend to expand slightly during flight. Recline your seat to a comfortable position. Lift the between-seat armrest to give yourself a little extra room if you have an empty seat next to you. Place an inflatable neck pillow around your neck, or use an airline pillow. Lean against the wall of the plane.

6 When the seatbelt sign is turned off, move about the cabin.
Walk and stretch in the galley area to keep your legs from stiffening and to prevent blood clots from forming.

7 When sleeping, insert cotton in your ears and place a moist handkerchief over your nose.
Low-level engine noise can disrupt sleep patterns. For better rest, filter out noise using sterile cotton instead of ear plugs, so the inner ear can adjust to cabin pressure changes. If sterile cotton is not available, use noise-canceling headphones connected to a tape or

CD player. A damp handkerchief over your nose will prevent your nasal passages from drying out. Block out as much of the light as possible. Close the window shade. Don an eye mask, or use an article of clothing (sweater, jacket, hat) as a blindfold.

8 Use deep-breathing techniques to relax.
Breathe in deeply through your nose, then out through your mouth. Focus only on the breaths you are taking—say to yourself, "Sleeeeeeeep. Sleeeeeeep. Sleeeeeep," as you inhale and exhale. Do not think about work, about your big meeting tomorrow, about how much you would rather be at home—think only about sleep.

Be Aware
Keep your seatbelt visible at all times. If your seatbelt is not in plain sight, you risk being awakened by the flight crew for a belt check.

Lost Luggage

1 File a report at the airport.
As soon as you realize your bags are missing, go immediately to the lost-luggage counter and file a report. Get a copy of the report, and write down the name of the person who helps you and the report number.

2 Obtain the direct phone number for the baggage counter.

Airport personnel may give you a toll-free number to call to check on the status of your bags. Take the number, but ask for the number of the lost-baggage counter at the airport itself.

3 Request compensation.

Some airlines will issue a check on the spot to cover the immediate cost of your buying clothing or essentials. Or the airline may give you a toiletries bag to cover your grooming needs until your bag is retained.

4 Call the airport baggage counter regularly.

Do not assume the airline will call you.

5 Be prepared for a two-day delay.

Do not assume that your bag will be put on the next departing flight to your destination: Airlines place recovered luggage only on their own planes, not on those of other carriers. If the next flight is not until late the following evening, you may not see your bag for two days.

6 Purchase necessary items before you leave the airport.

If you arrive at your destination on a holiday or late at night, you may not be able to shop for essentials in town.

how to survive a nightmare business trip

Be Aware

- If luggage is lost rather than just delayed, an airline's liability in the United States is limited to $1,250 per passenger, no matter how many bags have been lost. On international flights, the liability limit is about $9 per pound of checked baggage. Reimbursement may take months.

- To make your bag easier to spot, place a colored ribbon on the handle or a distinctive strap around the bag before checking it.

- Watch the bags as they come down the conveyer belt to the carousel, even if you do not have immediate access to it. You will be able to see if anyone else takes your bag.

- Write your name and the phone number of the place you will be staying for the first two days of your trip on two business cards. Place one inside your luggage and one in a card holder on the outside of your bag. (Never place your home address and phone in a visible identification tag. You do not want to advertise that you are away from home.)

- Dress for the worst—wear clothing on the plane that you can live in (and with) for two days. Anticipate that you might be giving your presentation or attending the meeting in what you are wearing on the plane.

- Carry essential medical and hygiene items, as well as any irreplaceable presentation materials, in your carry-on luggage.

Cheap Hotel

1 Request a room with a quiet location.
Avoid rooms near elevators, vending machines, the ice maker, the parking lot, or a noisy bar. Ask for a room at the end of the hall so there is less foot traffic outside the door.

2 Check the mechanicals and plumbing.
Before unpacking, check air conditioning, heat, television, lights, and water pressure. If any are not working properly or are otherwise unacceptable, request a new room.

3 Remove the bedspread.
Cheap hotels do not regularly clean bedspreads. Use towels for warmth. Call the front desk to request extra towels if there aren't enough in the room.

4 Clip the curtains closed.
If the curtains do not fully close, secure the two sides together using whatever you have on hand—paper or binder clips, tape, or pins and needles from a sewing kit.

5 Check the mattress firmness.
If the bed is too soft, place the mattress on the floor.

6 Check the clock.
Make sure the alarm is not set to go off in the middle of the night. Avoid the wake-up service—it is

notoriously unreliable in cheap hotels. Set the alarm clock, or carry a travel clock with an alarm.

7 Avoid the morning shower rush.
Cheap hotels may run out of hot water anytime between 7 and 9 A.M. Shower earlier or later.

Be Aware
- Travel with lightbulbs bright enough to use for reading.
- Travel with two small rubber doorstops. For security, wedge one firmly under the door to your room and the other under the door that adjoins the next room.
- Travel with snacks, including protein bars and instant hot cereal. Cheap hotels may have no restaurant, no in-room coffee, and no vending machines. Even if there is a restaurant, the food might be terrible.

Dull Town

★ Ask the locals for recommendations.
Ask the hotel clerk (or better yet, a porter) for a restaurant where you can "sample the local flavor." Most towns have at least one dish, restaurant, or tourist attraction that residents consider special.

★ Adopt an alias.
Pretend to be someone else when you go out. Be a secret service agent, an astronaut, a mime—whatever

your fantasy is. Pretend you have an accent. Cross-dressing is not recommended for all towns, however.

★ Do the opposite of everything you normally do.
If you usually go to bed early, stay out late. If you usually drink beer, drink coffee. Talk to the people you would normally ignore or avoid.

★ Play cards.
If none of the above works, obtain a deck of cards. Solitaire is a great time killer. Build a house of cards, or try to toss as many as you can across the room and into the wastebasket.

HOW TO ENHANCE YOUR STATURE

Pretend You Have an Assistant

★ Alter your outgoing voicemail message.
Ask a spouse or friend, preferably with an intriguing foreign accent, to record your outgoing message. It should be a version of the following: "You have reached the office of [*your name here*]. S/he is not available to take your call. Please leave a message and s/he will return your call as soon as possible."

★ Receive calls on your mobile phone.
While you are with someone you want to impress, either in an office conference room or at a restaurant, have a friend call you at a pre-arranged time. Answer the phone and say to the person with whom you are meeting, "Sorry, but I have to take this call. No one but my assistant has this number and I told him to call me only in emergencies."

★ Use a pager.
Subscribe to a paging service that alerts you with a beep for headlines or sports scores. Pretend the pages are from your assistant. In an exasperated voice, say, "It's my new assistant. He can't seem to do anything without my approval!"

★ Tip the host at a restaurant.
Tell the host to come to your table during the meal and say that you have an urgent phone call from your assistant.

ATTEND MEETINGS TO WHICH YOU ARE NOT INVITED

★ Ask the receptionist for a conference room reservation schedule.
Determine which meetings are worth crashing.

★ Choose meetings carefully.
Do not attend any meeting at which your direct supervisor is present. If your supervisor is out of the office, definitely attend the meeting and people will think you have been designated as a replacement. If your supervisor is in town, go to other departments' meetings.

★ Invent a reason for attending.
Approach the person running the meeting in advance and explain that you are attending for "professional development." The chairperson will most likely assume that there is some new Human Resources department program. Others attending the meeting will assume you are supposed to be there.

★ Bring snacks.
People will never question your attendance if you bring food.

how to enhance your stature

MOVE INTO AN UNOCCUPIED OFFICE

1   Take note of offices that have been vacant for a significant length of time.

2   Slowly take possession of an office.
Begin by working on a project in the office. If questioned, explain that you "needed a little peace and quiet in order to get [*project name*] done."

3   Occupy the office regularly.
For two weeks, spend at least an hour a day in the space, working on your project.

4   Expand your hours of occupancy.
After two weeks, begin leaving personal items and other files in the office.

5   Log onto the computer in the new office with your password.

6   Forward your phone calls.
Program your phone to send your calls to the extension in the new office.

7   Complain to the IT department.
Tell the Information Technologies department that your old extension still hasn't been transferred to your new phone.

8 Move your nameplate.
Place your nameplate on the new desk or in the slot outside the door, depending on company practice.

9 Close the door when working.
Look annoyed when anyone knocks or tries to come in. After approximately eight weeks of squatting, the office will be perceived as yours.

ALTER YOUR BUSINESS CARDS

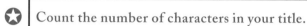 Count the number of characters in your title.
The new title you select needs to occupy roughly the same space on the card so that it doesn't float or appear obviously doctored. For example, "Editorial Assistant" can become "Editorial Director," but not simply "Editor" or "Senior Editor." Suggested replacements:
- "Marketing Manager" with "Marketing Director"
- "Assistant to the President" with "Assistant Vice-President"
- "Executive Secretary" with "Chief Exec. Officer."
- "Customer Service Rep." with "Customer Service Mgr."

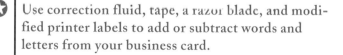 Use correction fluid, tape, a razor blade, and modified printer labels to add or subtract words and letters from your business card.

Use Props

★ Carry a briefcase.
Invest in a good-quality leather briefcase or attaché case and carry it at all times. When someone asks you for something, say, "Oh, I have it here in my brief-case." Consider a locking model for added stature.

★ Carry a fountain pen.
Fountain pens denote wealth and good breeding. Do not carry the pen in a pocket protector.

Look Busier than You Are

★ Purchase a headset and attach it to your phone.
It doesn't matter whether it's actually connected or not—tape it to the bottom of the phone if it won't hook in. Wear it constantly, and talk loudly when-ever someone passes by.

★ Keep large piles of paper on your desk at all times. Re-arrange the stacks occasionally.

★ Type furiously from time to time.
Position your monitor so the screen is not visible to anyone passing by or entering your space. Periodically, look intently at the monitor and type as fast as you can. Type nonsense, if you must—but do it at a speed of at least 70 words per minute.

chapter 3: on-the-job survival

★ Show up early and stay late.
You can maintain the same eight-hour day—just run your errands in the middle of the day. Few people will think twice about your absence from your desk in the middle of the day, but everyone will notice how early you get there and how late you leave. Long midday absences, if noticed, will be interpreted as business lunches, a sign of importance.

★ Muss your hair and look stressed whenever you pass your supervisor's office.

START A HELPFUL RUMOR

★ Receive messages from headhunters.
Have a friend, posing as a headhunter, make repeated calls to the receptionist. The friend should say, "I'm with [*official sounding name*] Headhunting Agency—may I speak with [*your name*]?" Word will likely get back to your supervisor.

★ Plant a reference check with the Human Resources department.
When the office is sure to be closed—late at night, on a weekend, or when you are certain everyone in the Human Resources department has left for the day—have a friend leave a voice-mail message saying he or she is checking references on [*your name*] and will call back later. The caller should not leave a return phone number nor a company name, but can leave their own name. The caller should sound casual but busy, as if

he or she is checking a list of names with a variety of employers.

★ Take the receptionist or your direct supervisor's assistant into your "confidence."
Explain that you are "entertaining" a position at another company, but that you "really want to stay." Ask for advice, knowing that word will get back to the boss.

★ Talk with people in other departments about forthcoming changes in your department.
Say you are not at liberty to reveal the whole story, but major changes will be coming. Ask if they know anything about future plans for your supervisor's parking place/office.

★ Conduct rumor-inducing conversations in public areas.
Spend time conversing at the water cooler, the lunchroom, bathroom, lobby, stairwells, elevators, and hallways. A loud whisper is most effective in getting people's attention. What you are talking about is not important: The fact that you are engaging in so many hushed conversations is the important factor.

HOW TO AVOID DOWNSIZING

Make Yourself Seem Indispensable

⭐ Perform thankless tasks.
Offer to do the billing, track vacation or comp time, sort the mail, answer the phones at lunchtime, replace the toner, or clean out the refrigerator. Master the jobs no one else wants.

⭐ Offer to organize office social events.
Do more than your share of planning office birthday parties and making sure everyone signs the card. Organize office parties, picnics, and holiday gatherings. Maintain a password-protected database of contacts and suppliers.

⭐ Get your name out.
Write an occasional article for the company newsletter or speak at a company event.

⭐ Become the key master.
Cultivate a collection of keys and codes for as many doors and drawers as possible. Store them in a locked place.

⭐ Be the one at meetings who says, "OK, let's get started."

★ Be the office handyperson.
Bring your tool kit to work and fix little problems around the office.

★ Propose ways to save the company money.
Suggest that employees use second-day postage rather than express; turn off lights in unused offices; re-use sticky notes; recycle memos, reports, and other documents internally by using the back side for scrap paper and drafts; insert "saving the resources of our company and our country" into every conversation; and remind your boss that "a dollar not spent goes right to the bottom line."

★ Start wearing glasses.
You will look more intelligent.

CHAPTER 4

WORKPLACE EMERGENCIES

HOW TO TREAT WORKPLACE INJURIES

Stapled Finger

1 Determine where the staple entered the finger.
If the staple is embedded in the fleshy pad of the finger, proceed to step 2. If the staple entered through the nail or the side of the finger, see Be Aware, page 120.

2 Obtain strong tweezers or needle-nose pliers.
If neither tool is available, use a flat-head screwdriver.

3 Place one side of the tip of the tool between the staple and the skin.
If using a screwdriver, place the tip under the staple.

4 Lift or pry the staple out.
With a fast, steady motion, close the tweezers or pliers and pull upward. The staple should be pulled straight out in the direction that it entered the finger. The staple will be in its original shape: The ends will be straight and should not cause further injury upon removal.

5 Wash the wound with soap and warm water.

6 Apply isopropyl alcohol or hydrogen peroxide.
Use a sterile cotton ball or a clean cloth to wipe on the disinfectant.

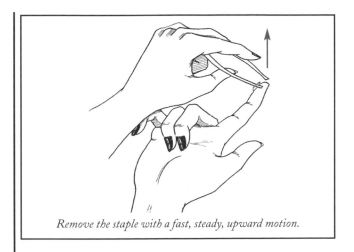

Remove the staple with a fast, steady, upward motion.

7 Apply pressure to the wound to stop residual bleeding.

8 Dress the wound with a bandage.

9 Examine the staple.
If the staple is not intact, a piece may still be in the wound and can cause pain, swelling, and infection. Seek medical help if any part of the staple remains in the finger.

10 Monitor the wound.
With or without a piece of the staple in it, a deep puncture wound may cause an infection. If the finger swells or remains painfully sore for more than 24 hours, see a healthcare professional.

Be Aware

- A staple that enters the finger through the nail can cause a small bone fracture or a bone infection (osteomyelitis). If the staple has punctured the nail, seek medical attention to rule out either of these conditions.
- A staple that enters the side of the finger can damage nerves, tendons, or blood vessels. If the staple is in the side of the finger, is especially deep, or causes numbness, it is best to seek professional help before removal.
- Tetanus bacteria, *Clostridium tetani,* can enter the body through a cut or puncture even if the penetrating object is not dirty or rusty. If you experience painful muscle spasms, lockjaw, difficulty swallowing, or difficulty breathing, seek medical attention immediately. To be safe, get a tetanus booster if you have not had one within five years.

DEEP-FRYER BURN

1 Take your hand out of the hot oil.
If the burn was caused by splattering oil, stand back from the deep fryer. Avoid touching the burned area.

2 Watch for flames.
Grease is highly combustible. Any oil above 400° to 600°F (200° to 300°C) may burst into flames and set fire to clothing. Smother any flames with wet oven mitts or wet towels to extinguish.

3 Plunge the burned area into cold running water.
Immerse the burn immediately and keep the hand or other body part under water until you are ready to apply the dressing.

4 Apply a dressing.
When the area is cool, cover it with a dry clean sheet or towel. Use a clean apron if nothing else is available.

5 Call emergency services.
While any burn the size of a dime or larger on the hands, feet, or face should be checked by a healthcare professional, a burn larger than a few inches across requires an immediate visit to the emergency room. Burn victims should always be transported by ambulance: Tell the emergency phone operator and emergency room attendant that you have a burn injury. If there is a burn center within 30 minutes, bypass other hospitals and seek specialized care.

Be Aware

- Because of the risk of damage to nerves and blood vessels, any circumferential burn (around an arm, leg, finger, or the entire body) should be treated at an emergency room immediately.
- Infection is not an immediate concern: Hot grease sterilizes the area temporarily.
- Do not put oils or other petroleum-based products on the burn.

Finger Cut on Deli Slicer

1 Turn off the slicer.
Use the power switch or yank out the cord. Yell for help if necessary.

2 Control the bleeding.
Locate a large, clean, absorbent cloth (a shirt or an apron is effective). Wrap the cloth around the injured finger and apply steady pressure with your other hand to stop the bleeding. Sit down and elevate the injured hand above the level of your heart. The fingers have a large number of blood vessels, so the blood loss may appear significant, but it probably is not.

3 Determine if part of the finger is missing.
Check (or ask a co-worker to check) the slicer for any missing piece of the finger. If part of the finger has been cut off, perform the following steps, then see "If Part of the Finger Has Been Amputated," page 124.

4 Maintain pressure.
Apply pressure on the finger for 5 minutes, then check the wound. If blood continues to spurt from the laceration, continue to apply pressure for 15 additional minutes. As the cloth becomes saturated, remove and replace it with a new one.

chapter 4: workplace emergencies

5 Clean the wound.

When the bleeding has slowed or stopped, examine the wound while gently rinsing it in a stream of cool tap water, taking care not to dislodge any visible blood clots.

6 Determine severity.

If the wound is through a finger joint or the nail bed, if part of the finger is attached to the hand by only skin, or if bone is visible, go to an emergency room; have a co-worker drive you. Bring additional towels and continue to apply pressure.

7 Cover and close the wound.

If the wound is less than half an inch in length, if you can move your finger normally, and if you can feel your fingertip, try to bring the skin edges of the wound together with pressure. Continue washing the wound under running tap water. Pat dry and re-apply direct pressure with a clean cloth to absorb any blood. Use an adhesive bandage to cover the wound and maintain the contact of the edges of the skin.

8 Get a tetanus shot.

If you have not had a tetanus booster in the last five years, get one as soon as possible.

IF **P**ART OF THE **F**INGER **H**AS **B**EEN **A**MPUTATED

1 Do not submerge the severed part.
The severed piece should not be placed in water, milk, or any other liquid.

2 Do not attempt to clean the severed part.
Cleaning the amputated piece may alter the character of the skin and other tissue that may be re-attached.

3 Prepare for transport.
Get a clean cloth or paper towel and soak it in cold running water. Wring to remove excess water and gently wrap the severed part in the towel.

4 Chill.
Place the bundled piece in a small bowl filled with ice. Cover the bundle with more ice. Do not let the part come into direct contact with ice.

5 Call emergency services.
Driving yourself, or having someone drive you, is not advisable if you or the driver are prone to fainting. Call an ambulance and bring the bowl containing the amputated part with you.

HOW TO RETRIEVE A CANDY BAR STUCK IN THE LUNCHROOM VENDING MACHINE

1 Wait several seconds.
Newer vending machines may be equipped with special technology that senses when an item has not dropped; the machine may return your money or give you another selection.

2 Purchase the item again.
Depending on how severely the snack is stuck and how much money you have, you may be able to jar it loose and get a second one by selecting the same item again.

3 Choose an item from the row above.
If your snack is stuck at an angle toward the glass at the end of the row, an item dropping from above may knock it free.

4 Jostle the machine.
Vending machines are extremely heavy and can cause major injury if they tip over. Carefully bang on the side of the machine. Do not hit glass areas.

Rock the machine forward and back slightly.

5 Rock the machine.
Tip the machine backward very slightly (not side-to-side) and let it drop back in place to jar the item loose. Do not press on the glass.

6 Push in the vending door and remove the candy.
Once the item—or items—have dropped, reach in and slowly extricate it.

Be Aware
Anti-theft devices make it virtually impossible to reach in and up past the vending door. Do not risk getting your arm stuck in the machine.

HOW TO THWART A LUNCH THIEF

1 Prepare a special lunch bag.
Staple your lunch bag shut. This will send the thief who has been stealing your lunch a not-so-subtle message that you know what he is up to. Write your name on the bag in large block letters to prevent the thief from claiming a bag mix-up.

2 Track the items stolen.
A clever thief will not risk being caught red-handed with your entire lunch bag; he will simply remove his favorite items. Assess the thief's appetite and level of sophistication by observing for several days what items are taken and when. If the labeled and stapled bag does not deter him, you are dealing with a dedicated thief.

3 Set a trap.
Once you have determined the thief's method and preferences, alter your lunch accordingly. If the thief likes sandwiches, hide a layer of well-chopped jalapeño peppers between the other ingredients (cover with a thin layer of mayonnaise, if necessary). If the thief prefers cookies, cupcakes, or other sweets, sprinkle a layer of cayenne pepper on the underside of these items. These traps will teach the thief a lesson and may flush the thief out into the open (wait by the water cooler later) if you are unable to catch him in the act.

Wait until the thief has removed the item from your lunch bag.

chapter 4: workplace emergencies

4 | Monitor the refrigerator.
Find a surveillance spot with a clear view of the office kitchen or stroll past once every few minutes. Mid- to late-morning is the prime time for lunch theft. Each time someone goes to the refrigerator, listen for the sound of your bag being ripped open. If there is no ripping sound, check the staples after each person leaves. Resume hiding until you hear a ripping sound or you see someone with his back to you, peeking into the refrigerator for a longer than usual time.

5 | Wait for the crinkle.
Listen attentively until you hear the thief open your bag and remove an item; if you move too soon you risk the defense of simple bag confusion.

6 | Pounce.
As the thief turns away from the fridge with your lunch item, jump out from your hiding spot. Say, "I believe that's my lunch you have in your hand!" If the thief denies that the item is from your lunch bag, show him the now-unsealed bag and explain that it was sealed before he opened the refrigerator door. If he still professes innocence, tell him to prove it by taking a large bite of the (doctored) item.

HOW TO SPOT A SHOPLIFTER

1 Watch for attentive behavior.
Most shoppers are absorbed in the browsing process and oblivious to their surroundings. Shoplifters will look around and be highly attuned to the proximity of others.

2 Observe movements.
Shoplifters often have a rigid posture and a strained expression. They avoid making eye contact and make quick, jerky movements as they conceal pilfered items.

3 Look for bulges.
Shoplifters may keep a folded bag under their shirt or jacket, or may be carrying a near-empty bag from the same store. Once shoplifters begin acquiring merchandise, they may put on several layers of clothing and fill the bags they are carrying.

4 Watch from above.
If the store has multiple, open floors, observe from a higher vantage point. Alternatively, stand behind a rack of clothing and peer between garments. Do not attempt to look under or above the walls of dressing rooms unless such surveillance is acceptable store policy.

chapter 4: workplace emergencies

bulging pockets

multiple layers

bulging bag

Watch for bulges.

How to Thwart a Shoplifter

1 Keep items well organized.
Thieves thrive on disorganization and will take advantage of unshelved stock. Fold clothes well and make sure each pile has the same style and an identical number of items. A quick glance will tell you if something is missing.

2 Employ defensive merchandising.
Do not shelve the newest, trendiest, or most expensive items right by the door where a thief can grab something and run.

3 Make your presence known.
Shoplifters do not want to stand out and be noticed. Regularly walk the floor, make eye contact, and offer to help customers.

4 Monitor changing rooms.
Track the number of items a shopper brings into (and takes out of) the changing room by keeping all rooms empty of merchandise and clean of tags, pins, and labels. Check the room after the shopper exits and make sure all items are accounted for.

HOW TO SURVIVE IF TRAPPED IN ...

If kicking or banging on the door to the **bathroom, supply closet, walk-in-freezer,** or **lion cage** does not summon help immediately, save your energy for other means of egress.

A BATHROOM

BREAK THROUGH THE WALL

1 Tap on the wall until you hear a hollow sound. Wall studs are 16 inches apart. The hollow sound indicates the space between the studs.

Bang a hole in the wall large enough to crawl through.

2 Bang a hole in the wall.
Use a wooden plunger handle or other strong bathroom implement to poke at the wall. Avoid tiled areas. Continue jabbing and breaking the wall until you have opened a wide hole.

3 Crawl through.
Squeeze your body between the studs.

CLIMB OUT THROUGH THE CEILING
1 Push out the ceiling tiles.
Stand on the sink or other sturdy fixture. Push several drop-tile squares up and over to the side.

2 Look for pipes or other handholds.

3 Select a horizontal pipe that leads out of the bathroom.

4 Pull yourself up and onto the pipe.
Grab a pipe at least 6 inches in diameter. Pull up as you would for a chin-up, then swing your legs onto the pipe. Do not put your weight on the ceiling tiles or you risk falling through.

5 Crawl.
Shimmy along the pipe until you are no longer above the bathroom.

6 Kick out a ceiling tile and drop down into the hallway.

Stand on the sink and pull yourself up on a pipe.

Be Aware

With ready access to water from the sink, you should be able to survive for days, if not weeks, in the bathroom, even without food.

how to survive if trapped in . . .

A Supply Closet

1 Find a screwdriver.
If no screwdriver is available, look for a letter opener, bottle opener, tape dispenser, cocktail shaker, three-hole punch, or other metal implement with a flat end. A metal pen or strong plastic pen can also work.

2 Examine the door hinges.
Most doors open in and have the hinges on the inside. Locate the lower hinge.

3 Place the tip of the screwdriver under the top edge of the hinge pin.

Remove the hinge pins from the door.

4 Push or bang on the top of the handle of the screwdriver.
Pound with a hammer, shoe heel, table or chair leg, or other hard, unbreakable object.

5 Remove the pin from the hinge.

6 Remove the upper hinge.
Repeat steps 3 through 5.

7 Lift the door away from the door frame.
Pull on the hinge side first. You may be able to pull the door completely away from the frame.

8 Exit.

A WALK-IN FREEZER

1 Stay calm.
Panic wastes energy, which is warmth. The room's insulation and motor noise will likely prevent anyone from hearing your cries for help. Find a metal implement (keys or coins will work) and tap several times on the door to get someone's attention.

2 Check the door and lock area.
By law, all walk-in freezers and refrigerators must have an emergency release switch on the interior. Look on the door for a fluorescent knob that turns, or a lever that moves up and down.

3 Locate a power switch.
Most units have a temperature control module on the inside, but it is likely to be well protected and may require tools to access. Some models may have an accessible on/off switch. If you can access the switch, turn off the cooling element.

4 Locate boxes.
Tear cardboard boxes apart and spread the cardboard on the floor. The freezer's floor will be concrete or metal, and coming in contact with it will reduce your body temperature quickly.

5 Look for insulating materials.
Many food items are packed in paper, plastic, foam peanuts, or straw. Lie down on the cardboard and cover yourself with insulating items to preserve body heat. Take care to cover your head completely: In cold conditions, an enormous amount of heat is lost through the head.

6 Breathe slowly and stay put.
Take slow breaths and do not move around in the freezer or overexert yourself.

7 Stay hydrated.
Suck on ice cubes or on frost from food parcels. Do not use body heat to melt frozen items or you risk hypothermia.

Use cardboard for insulation.

8 Eat only if ice is available.

Digestion requires water, so do not eat unless there is a sufficient supply of ice for you to melt. Eat ice cream or other foods intended to be eaten frozen. Avoid meats; these are likely to be frozen solid anyway.

9 Tap on the door every 15 minutes until help arrives.

Be Aware

- Do not attempt to disable the refrigeration mechanism. This may cause the unit to malfunction and leak noxious chemicals.
- Remain close to the ground. Although in most environments heat rises, the freezer will have a uniform temperature throughout, and the refrigeration mechanism is likely to be closer to the ceiling than at floor level.
- It is often customary to don a fur or other warm coat before entering a commercial freezer for any length of time. If you are wearing a coat, use it, but avoid over-exertion as you move around: Sweating causes the body to cool rapidly. If you feel yourself begin to sweat, open the coat slightly.
- Do not build a fire in an enclosed space.

A Lion Cage

If the Lion Is Not Immediately Visible

1 Quickly survey the cage.

Check to see if the lion is present. Most zoos have a large outdoor area for the lions to roam, and the lion may have wandered outside. The cage will be connected to this area through a small passage with a door that allows the cage to be sealed and cleaned while the lion is outside.

chapter 4: workplace emergencies

2 Shut the door.
If a door is present and the lion is not, shut the door. If the lion is present, do not shut the door.

3 Yell for help.

If the Lion Is Visible
1 Do not run.
Even if the cage is large, or you feel you can safely make it to the passageway and through the door to the outdoor area, do not turn and run. This will only get the lion's attention, and there may be more lions outside.

2 Stay still and calm.
Do not provoke the lion by moving around, running, or charging.

3 Check for cubs.
A lioness guarding cubs will defend them fiercely, and may be more inclined to attack. If you see cubs, freeze.

4 Check for food.
Lions are extremely protective of food, and even a lion with a full belly will protect his "kill." If the lion appears to be feeding or you notice fresh meat, do not approach the lion or its food.

5 Observe the lion's eyes and tail.
A lion in a zoo will be desensitized to the presence of humans and may not attack immediately. Lions have different temperaments, however, and can range from

how to survive if trapped in . . .

passive to highly aggressive. Even a passive lion is likely to eventually attack a stranger in its cage. If the lion meets your gaze and its tail begins to twitch, the lion is getting ready to attack.

6 Listen for a growl.
A low staccato growl, combined with eye contact and a lashing tail, usually indicates that an attack is likely.

7 Find a defensive tool.
Moving very slowly, pick up anything within reach: a water bowl, bench, or anything else that may be used to fend off a charge.

8 Back away slowly.
Moving carefully, back toward the door of the cage. Using a quiet but firm voice, tell someone to open the cage or, if impossible, to get the lion keeper immediately.

9 Watch for mock charges.
A lion may make several "mock" charges before actually attacking. It will run forward suddenly, then stop. It may back away before charging again. Mock-charging is an indication that a real attack is imminent. Stand your ground and be ready.

10 Yell.
Yell as loud as you can. Lions are sensitive to loud noises and yelling may discourage one from further charges.

Watch for signs of imminent attack: twitching tail, eye contact, and growling.

11 Fend off attack.
If the lion attacks, use a bench, bowl, or any other object to push its paws and head away from you.

12 Yell for help.
Keep screaming as loudly as possible.

HOW TO REMOVE A TIE CAUGHT IN THE DOCUMENT FEEDER

1 Determine how quickly you will need to act.
If your breathing is constricted, do not hesitate—cut the tie off quickly (see step 5). You may be able to reduce some of the constriction by getting as close to the feeder as possible.

2 If your breathing is not restricted, try pulling the tie. Use firm but steady pressure. Do not yank: If the document feeder uses gear-driven rollers, you may strip the gears or tear the tie. If the feeder is particularly powerful, you may be unable to pull the tie out.

3 Turn off the copier.
If you can reach the power switch, turn it off. Alternatively, yank or kick out the power cord.

4 Search the area for a cutting implement.
Copier areas often house scissors, utility knives, paper cutters, and other devices you might use to cut the tie free. Open the copier supply door and look in there. Feel around on nearby tables and inside nearby cabinets for useful items.

Turn off machine; cut the tie or call for help.

5 Make a single fast cut across the tie at its shortest visible point.
Pull the tie taut with your neck or free hand, and slice through it quickly.

6 Call for help if you cannot fix the situation yourself.
Cry out for help. If a phone is within reach, call the receptionist or a co-worker.

7 If help does not arrive and no cutting implement is available, try to detach the feeder unit.
Often, the feeder unit simply snaps onto the top of the copier. You may be able to lift it off its hinges.

HOW TO FIX A DENTED COMPANY VEHICLE

Dents can be fixed by either pushing out the dent from behind or pulling on it from the front. The latter is more difficult, but may be your only hope if you cannot access the back of the dented panel.

1 Check the location of the dent.
Dents on quarter panels, trunks, hoods, and fenders are relatively easy to fix. If the dent is in the door or on the roof, or if the dent is very sharp or deep, see "Make a Glue Puller," page 148.

2 Access the rear of the panel.
If the dent is on the hood or trunk, open the hood or trunk to access the back of the panel. If the dent is on a fender, remove the plastic liner panel (which may require removing plastic screws) to gain access to the sheet metal. If the dent is on a quarter panel, pull back the carpet or trunk liner until you see the metal plate.

3 Push out the dent with your hand.
Press firmly but gently. For better results, use a golf ball, baseball, or other hard, round object to push out the dent. Small dents will require greater pressure. Do not push too hard or you will create a dent in the other direction; sheet metal on cars is very thin.

chapter 4: workplace emergencies

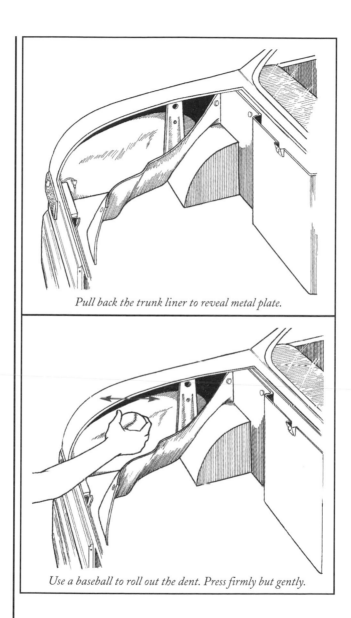

Pull back the trunk liner to reveal metal plate.

Use a baseball to roll out the dent. Press firmly but gently.

Make a Glue Puller

You will need: hot-glue gun, wood-glue sticks (amber, not white), denatured alcohol, and a dowel rod (2 inches by 18 to 24 inches long).

1 Insert a glue stick into the glue gun.

2 Plug in the glue gun.
Allow the gun to heat for 5 to 10 minutes.

3 Clean the dent.
Use a clean cloth to rub alcohol on the dent to strip any wax from the area and ensure a good bond.

4 Coat the dowel rod with glue.
Cover a 1-inch section at the tip of the dowel rod with the melted glue.

5 Press the dowel into the dent.
Immediately place the glue-covered end of the dowel rod into the center of the dented area. Hold it very still against the steel for 1 to 2 minutes or until the glue is dry. Do not wiggle the dowel rod or you will break the bond.

6 Yank the dowel rod.
Use a single swift, hard motion to pull the dent out. The dowel should also pull free of the car.

7 Repeat, if necessary.

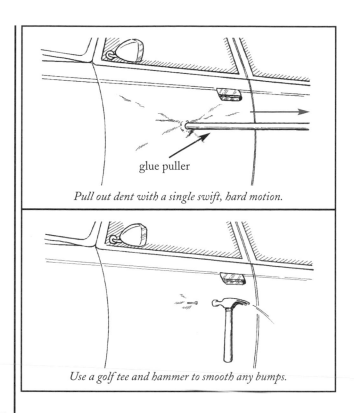

Pull out dent with a single swift, hard motion.

Use a golf tee and hammer to smooth any bumps.

8 Smooth out any bumps.
If you pulled too hard and there is now a bump, flatten the high spot by placing the tip of a golf tee over the bulge. Tap a hammer against the wide end of the tee until the bump is flush. This method should not remove the paint.

9 Remove excess glue.
Pour alcohol on a clean cloth and rub the panel to remove any glue that remains.

HOW TO RESTORE A SHREDDED DOCUMENT

1 Determine the identifying characteristics of the document.

Use paper color and weight, distinctive type fonts, illustrations, and logos to establish which is the document you are trying to restore. Find an unshredded document or letter from the same sender as a model.

2 Sort the shreds.

Using the identifying characteristics of the stationery, and comparing the angle of the edges of each shred, begin to organize the shred strips. Separate and discard shreds from other documents until all remaining shreds are from the target document.

3 Begin paste-up.

Place the first shred vertically on your paste-up board (a whiteboard works well) using clear, removable tape. Using the same orientation, place a second shred alongside the first. Compare it against one side, then the other. If it is a match, tape it down next to the original shred. If it is not, lightly tape it down an inch away, parallel to the first strip.

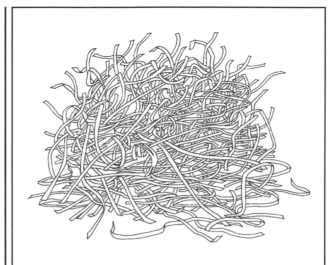

Sort shreds by distinctive color, type, and design. Discard shreds not from target document.

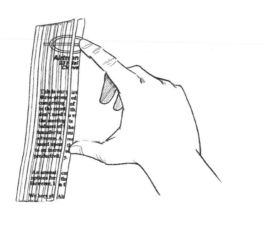

Tape each shred in place to re-assemble document.

4 Repeat.

Continue comparing strips. Keep the "raw" (uncompared) strips separate from the "rejected" (compared but non-matching) strips. If you run out of room, use a second paste-up board. Join matching strips as soon as the match is discovered.

5 Copy the reconstituted document.

When the document is re-assembled, sandwich taped strips between two sheets of clear overhead projector film or clear contact paper and photocopy.

Be Aware

- A three-page document will have 100 to 200 shred strips, and reassembly will take 1 to 2 hours, depending on skill level.
- Cross shredders, which shred documents in both directions, make salvage virtually impossible.

HOW TO UNCLOG
THE OFFICE TOILET
WITHOUT A PLUNGER

1 Wait several minutes.
Often clogs will resolve themselves with time.

2 Prepare more water.
Hold a full pitcher of water three feet above the rim of the bowl.

3 Pour and flush.
Pour the water into the bowl as you flush the toilet. The added water and pressure increases the force of the flush.

4 Check the bowl.
If it is still clogged, continue.

5 Get a wire coat hanger.
Untwist the hanger until it is relatively straight.

6 Tie a small hand towel to the hanger.
Create a loop at one end of the hanger to give you a better grip. Tie the hand towel in a knot at the other end. The knot should be approximately the same size as the opening at the bottom of the bowl. Make another small loop in the hanger just below the towel to prevent it from sliding off.

7 | Push the hanger through the clog.
Continue pushing as far as you can.

8 | Plunge.
Move the hanger up and down and in small circles to clear the clog.

9 | Withdraw the hanger.

10 | Flush.
If the clog does not clear, wait 10 minutes, then repeat steps 7 through 10. If the water level in the bowl remains high and close to the rim, do not try to flush the toilet.

If Pushing the Handle Does Not Flush the Toilet

1 | Remove the toilet tank lid.
If the toilet does not have a tank—often the case with high-pressure toilets in office buildings—do not try to fix a non-flushing toilet. Just leave and call maintenance.

2 | Check the back of the handle.
The handle should be connected inside the tank to one end of the "lift chain," or to a thin rod (float arm) connected to the chain. At its other end, the lift chain should be connected to the toilet flapper. One of the connections is most likely broken.

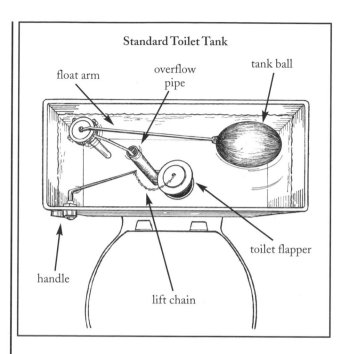

Standard Toilet Tank

float arm

overflow pipe

tank ball

handle

toilet flapper

lift chain

3 Turn off the water.

Turn the water off at the valve just below the tank. Put on a pair of thick rubber gloves.

4 Pull up the lift chain.

Tank water may be contaminated with waste if the trap seal is broken. Using your gloved hand or a hanger, pull up the chain. The toilet will flush. If the water supply is still on, the tank will begin filling quickly, so you will need to work fast.

5 Re-connect the flapper and chain.
Attach the chain to the handle using a paperclip, safety pin, or twist tie.

6 Turn the water back on.

7 Wash your hands thoroughly.
Use antibacterial soap or hydrogen peroxide.

Be Aware
Occasionally the toilet will not flush because the flapper has become dislodged and is not seating properly, causing the water to keep running into the bowl and the tank to remain empty. Jiggle the handle slightly to reseat the flapper properly.

HOW TO ESCAPE A STOCKROOM AVALANCHE

1 Position your head on your chest.
Immediately move your head down, touching your chin to your chest, as soon as you hear shelves creaking or detect objects falling.

2 Protect your head.
Bring your arms up over your head. Clasp your hands together behind your head and bring your elbows together in front of you. Keep your chin down and your arms over your head at all times.

3 Run toward the door.
If you see a relatively clear path of escape, proceed to the door as quickly as possible.

4 Find a safe spot.
If you cannot escape the room, move to the center of the floor, away from shelves, or take cover near shelves holding softer items.

5 Drop and curl.
Lie down and assume the fetal position, with your arms covering your head. Allow lighter, lower objects to cover you and give you protection from heavier objects falling from higher shelves.

Run.

How to Extricate Yourself from an Avalanche

1 | Move slowly.
Crawl on your hands and knees, maintaining a low profile. Expect a secondary slide. Avoid sudden movements that may cause precariously perched items to fall.

2 | Check for injuries.
Feel your arms, legs, torso, and hands. Wiggle your toes, flex your fingers, and bend your arms and legs slightly. Make sure nothing is broken before you get up.

3 | Move debris.
Push fallen items to the side. Be careful not to jar shelves or you risk another slide.

4 | Stand up.
Step over and around items and make your way to the door.

5 | Exit the stockroom.
Do not slam the door. Warn others of the danger.

HOW TO CLEAN UP A SPILL IN AISLE SEVEN

1 Stay with the spill.
Monitor the area from the moment you discover it.

2 Examine the spilled item.
A spill will be "dry," "wet," or "wet with glass." Determine which type you are facing.

3 Announce the spill.
Shout, "Wet spill with glass, aisle seven." Ask the employee who responds to remain with the spill while you get cleaning materials.

4 Prepare the cleaning supplies.
Bring a broom, dustpan, and rolling garbage can with bag if the spill is dry. If the spill is wet or wet with glass, also get two caution signs, rubber gloves, paper towels, a rag mop, and a filled bucket with ringer. Add an all-purpose cleaning agent to the water.

5 Prepare the spill area.
Place a caution sign on either side of a wet spill. Keep your bucket clear of the spilled material to avoid leaving tracks when you move it.

Use short, back and forth strokes. Rinse frequently.

6 | Remove the glass pieces and sweep.
Wearing the rubber gloves, pick up all noticeable glass shards and place them in the garbage bag. (Use paper towels if no gloves are available.) Sweep as much of the spilled item into the dustpan as possible and dump in the garbage can.

7 | Mop.
Thoroughly soak the mop head. Mop using short, back-and-forth strokes until no spillage remains. Avoid wide strokes, which will spread the spilled item. Dunk the mop head in the water frequently and wring thoroughly.

8 | Check the floor.
Some items (spaghetti sauce, for example) may stain floor surfaces. If you cannot remove the stain by mopping, leave a message for the night cleaning staff to clean and buff the area.

9 | Leave the signs in place.

10 | Wait 20 minutes, then check the spill area.
Remove the signs when the floor is dry.

Be Aware
Sticky items like soda, juice, and syrup or slippery items like oil, salad dressing, and concentrated detergent may require extra-thorough mopping.

APPENDIX

JARGON BINGO

Photocopy the Jargon Bingo cards on this spread, cut along the dotted lines, and take the cards with you to your next meeting. Keep one for yourself, and give the others to colleagues. Check off each word or phrase as it is used during the meeting. If you complete a row (across, up and down, or diagonally), you've won! Signal your fellow players by flipping your pen in the air and touching your index finger to your nose.

brand management	optimize	buzz	guerilla	no-brainer
takeaway	zero-sum	outside the box	slippery slope	team player
killer app	do the heavy lifting	★	ballpark	step up to the plate
up the flagpole	fast track	outsource	tipping point	viral
metrics	big picture	put to bed	downmarket	paradigm shift

blue sky	dog and pony show	game plan	merch	deliverable
upmarket	synergize	quality-driven	check with accounting	empower
facilitate	brainstorm	★	backburner	marketing hook
value-driven	fast track	impulse priced	profit-driven	win-win
user friendly	proactive	counter-intuitive	revisit	incentivize

re-prioritize	quality-driven	crash	big picture	brainstorm
team player	test case	perceived value	zero-sum	empower
ballpark	facilitate	★	repurpose	brand management
market-driven	backburner	optimize	check with legal	no-brainer
slippery slope	outside the box	fast track	takeaway	upmarket

THE "I QUIT" LETTER

Dear [*your boss's name*],

During the **years / months / days** that I have worked here, I've come to better understand my own needs and the needs of the company. Regrettably, I've reached the conclusion that these needs are no longer in synch.

Without any blame or bad feelings / For personal reasons I'd rather not discuss / On advice from my psychiatrist and lawyer, I've decided to tender my resignation. This is not a decision I've made lightly nor in haste. I want you to know that my departure has nothing to do with the fact that **I am over-worked and under-paid / you promoted that idiot instead of me / the company is severely dysfunctional and evil.**

It's just that I want to **spend more time in a job I feel I can grow in / work with people I respect while doing something worthwhile / get out before everyone gets indicted.**

I sincerely want to thank you for **giving me the opportunity to work with you / providing a job that allowed me to discover what I didn't want to do / nothing.**

I wish you the best of luck in the future, and hope we'll have a chance to cross paths again in **the future / the very, very distant future / court.**

Sincerely,
[*your name*]

The Experts

How to Identify a Nightmare Workplace
Source: Eileen Levitt is president of the HR Team (www.thehrteam.com), a company that specializes in employee communications, training, recruitment and retention strategies, and executive/employee coaching.

How to Get a Job You're Not Qualified For
Sources: Ian B. Maksik, "America's Service Guru" (www.usawaiter.com), conducts seminars and training courses in the hospitality industry around the world. • Peter Post is the great-grandson of Emily Post and an expert in business and personal etiquette. He is the co-author of *Etiquette Advantage in Business* and director of the Emily Post Institute (www.emilypost.com) in Burlington, Vermont. • Carole Martin (www.interviewcoach.com) is the interview coach at Monster.com. She holds a master's degree in Career Development and coaches MBA students on interviewing techniques at the Haas School of Business at the University of California at Berkeley. • R. J. Meagher, M.D., is a neurosurgeon in private practice at JRCT Neurosurgical Associates in Reading, Pennsylvania. • Seth Haplea, M.D., is a neurologist with a private practice in West Grove, Pennsylvania. • Leslie Hafter is an area manager with T. Williams Consulting, a management consulting firm that specializes in human capital solutions. • Franklin Lever, principal of Franklin Consulting Fork Lift Specialists (www.frankcon.qpg.com), has 36 years of experience providing solutions to forklift problems, including driver training and expert witness services in

forklift-related litigation. • LaVonda Henderson is a former shoe sales associate at Payless ShoeSource, Inc.

How to Survive the Interview
Sources: Carole Martin. • Leslie Hafter.

How to Disguise a Tattoo
Source: Sherry Maysonave is the author of *Casual Power: How to Power Up Your Nonverbal Communication and Dress Down for Success* and the founder and president of Empowerment Enterprises (www.casualpower.com), a consulting firm specializing in communication and image.

CHAPTER 2: PEOPLE SKILLS

How to Deal with a Nightmare Boss
Sources: Jan Yager, Ph.D. (www.janyager.com) is a sociologist, consultant, speaker, and author of *Business Protocol: How to Survive & Succeed in Business*. • *The Diagnostic and Statistical Manual of Mental Disorders,* Fourth Edition. • Leslie Hafter. • Johnathan Lazear lectures on the topic of workaholism and is the author of *Meditations for Men Who Do Too Much* and *The Man Who Mistook His Job for a Life*.

How to Deal with a Nightmare Co-Worker
Source: Jan Yager. • *The Diagnostic and Statistical Manual of Mental Disorders,* Fourth Edition.

How to Deal with a Nightmare Customer
Sources: Dianne Lancaster is the founder of the Anger Management Institute (www.manageanger.com) in Boulder, Colorado, and the author of *When Anger Is in Control*. She consults on stress management and anger in schools, the workplace, and the home. • Ian B. Maksik.

How to Survive the Office Picnic
Source: Phyllis Cambria is a celebrations expert and co-author with Patty Sachs of *The Complete Idiot's Guide to Throwing a Great Party*. She has organized hundreds of events for groups of 2 to 10,000. Cambria and Sachs own PartyPlansPlus.com, an online event planning, marketing, and party products company.

How to Make an Impromptu Toast
Source: Alfred Herzing is president of Toastmasters International (www.toastmasters.org), a nonprofit organization dedicated to helping its members improve their communication and leadership skills.

How to Survive a Workplace Romance
Source: Barbara Pachter (www. pachter.com) is a business communications and protocol specialist and the author of several books, including *When the Little Things Count . . . And They Always Count.*

CHAPTER 3: ON-THE-JOB SURVIVAL

How to Survive in a Tiny Workspace
Sources: Christopher R. Ryan is the creator of the Cubicle Survival Kit, a set of essential items for improving the cubicle experience, and CubeGuy.com, which offers survival strategies for cube dwellers. • Steve Hayes is the CEO and managing director of Outside In, an 11-year-old company specializing in the sale of lights to treat various body-clock problems. • Fred Lapp, a trucker for 17 years, currently hauls machinery and other freight east of the Mississippi. • John Ammons hauls lumber and other freight for Penske Trucking in eastern Ohio. • Max Heine is editorial director for *Overdrive, Truckers News*, and eTrucker.com. • Ed DeLozier, executive director of

the E-470 Public Highway Authority in Aurora, Colorado, served as a toll collector on the New Jersey Turnpike for 9 years. • Angus Kress Gillespie, Ph.D., a professor of American Studies at Rutgers University, is the co-author of *Looking for America on the New Jersey Turnpike,* a history of the roadway and its workers. • W. R. (Ross) Jennings III is the president of Cushing Manufacturing, a fabricator of toll booths and other commercial metal structures, in Richmond, Virginia.

How to Sneak Out of a Meeting

Sources: Peter Earnest, a former CIA field operative, spent 20 years in the agency's Clandestine Service in Europe and the Middle East. He currently serves as executive director of the International Spy Museum (www.spymuseum.org) in Washington, D.C. • The National Safety Council.

How to Cover Your Mistakes

Sources: Chris Pirillo is co-author of *Poor Richard's E-mail Publishing* and manages Lockergnome.com, a series of electronic publications. • Virginia Mattingly is a middle school teacher and co-author of *The Field Guide to Stains.* • Ian B. Maksik. • Steven Tamaccio owns Estetica Salons in Philadelphia and Wayne, Pennsylvania. He has been a hairdresser for 25 years and has his own line of hair-care products.

How to Survive If You Are Caught Slacking

Source: David Wiskus is a writer, musician, and founder of SlackersGuild.com, an online community for slackers of all stripes.

How to Survive a Nightmare Business Trip

Sources: Marybeth Bond (www.womentraveltips.com) is a travel expert/spokesperson, motivational speaker, television and radio commentator, and author of five books, including *A Woman's World* and *Gutsy Women*. • Drew Dimond is the president of the International Society of Hospitality Consultants and a 30-year veteran of the hotel and hospitality industries. He is also president of Dimond Hospitality Consulting Group (www.dimondconsultinggroup.com). • Bob Rosner is the author of *The Boss's Survival Guide* and *Working Wounded*, and the founder of RetentionEvangelist.com. He has 2 million frequent flyer miles and most people feel he needs to get a life. • Diana Fairechild (www.flyana.com) is an expert witness and speaker and the author of *Noni* as well as *Jet Smart* and *Jet Smarter*, which help airline passengers cope with the physical, emotional, and spiritual stresses of flying. She spent 21 years as a flight attendant, logging more than 10 million air miles.

How to Enhance Your Stature
Source: Bob Rosner.

How to Avoid Downsizing
Source: Bob Rosner.

CHAPTER 4: WORKPLACE EMERGENCIES

How to Treat Workplace Injuries
Sources: Seth Haplea. • Ken Zafren, M.D., F.A.C.E.P., is an emergency physician who lives in Anchorage, Alaska. He serves as medical director of Emergency Medical Services for the state of Alaska and is on the faculty at Stanford University Medical Center. • Melisa W. Lai, M.D., is a clinical chief resident in Emergency Medicine at the Harvard Affiliated Emergency Medicine Residency Program at Massachusetts General Hospital-Brigham & Women's Hospital-Mt. Auburn.

How to Retrieve a Candy Bar Stuck in the Lunchroom Vending Machine
Source: D & S Vending Inc. (www.dsvendinginc.com) sells and services vending machines in Cleveland, Ohio.

How to Thwart a Lunch Thief
Source: Bob Rosner.

How to Spot a Shoplifter
Source: Chris E. McGoey (www.crimedoctor.com) has been in security management for 30 years. He is a consultant and frequent lecturer on security and loss prevention.

How to Survive If Trapped in . . .
Sources: Michael Griffin (www.escapeguy.com) has escaped from prison cells, steel coffins, and from 25 pounds of chains and locks at the bottom of the Pacific Ocean. • Bill Stompf, sales manager at Bally Refrigerated Boxes (www.ballyrefboxes.com) in Morehead City, North Carolina, has worked in commercial refrigeration for 30 years. • Ken Zafren. • Michael Hackenberger runs the Bowmanville Zoological Park (www.bowmanvillezoo.com), Canada's oldest private zoo. He has bred and trained lions for 20 years, and his cats have appeared in such films as *George of the Jungle* and *The Ghost and the Darkness*. • Gareth Patterson, author and environmentalist (www.garethpatterson.com), has dedicated most of his adult life to the preservation of the African lion and its wilderness home.

How to Remove a Tie Caught in the Document Feeder
Source: Larry Raisch has worked with photocopiers for 30 years as a manufacturer, technician, technical manager, and service representative.

How to Fix a Dented Company Vehicle
Source: Brian Jump is president of the Superior Auto
Institute (www.nodents.com) and has 22 Paintless
Dent Repair schools worldwide.

How to Restore a Shredded Document
Source: C.J. Bronstrup (www.InvestigatorWebs.com),
retired owner of Atlas Investigations, specialized in
information gathering and skip tracing. He currently
provides marketing services and websites for private
investigators.

How to Unclog the Office Toilet Without a Plunger
Sources: Mike Carlin is a master plumber and principal of MC Associates (www.mcassociates.com), a
plumbing and HVAC contractor in Massachusetts. •
John Turmel, a master plumber, is the owner of Turmel
Plumbing, with locations in Corpus Christi, Austin,
and Fort Worth, Texas.

How to Escape a Stockroom Avalanche
Sources: James Li, M.D., practices and teaches in the
Division of Emergency Medicine at Harvard Medical
School in Cambridge, Massachusetts. He is an instruc-
tor for the American College of Surgeons' course for
physicians, Advanced Trauma Life Support. • John
Simonetti is an astronomer and Associate Professor of
Physics at Virginia Tech in Blacksburg, Virginia.

How to Clean Up a Spill in Aisle Seven
Source: Christian Quickle is a front-end manager at
the Columbus Boulevard Super Fresh Superstore in
Philadelphia, Pennsylvania.

ABOUT THE AUTHORS

JOSHUA PIVEN, a writer and former cubicle dweller, enjoys working in his pajamas until noon and celebrating "take yourself to lunch day." He is the co-author, with David Borgenicht, of *The Worst-Case Scenario Survival Handbook* series and lives in Philadelphia with his wife, Christine.

DAVID BORGENICHT is a writer, editor, husband, and working father who has been a shoe salesman, door-to-door canvasser, dishwasher, and pool boy in his working life. He is the co-author, with Joshua Piven, of all of the books in *The Worst-Case Scenario Survival Handbook* series, and of *The Action Hero's Handbook* (Quirk Books) with his brother, Joe. He lives in Philadelphia with his family (by night) and his employees (by day).

BRENDA BROWN is a freelance illustrator and cartoonist whose work has been published in many books and major publications, including *The Worst-Case Scenario Survival Handbook* series, *Esquire*, *Reader's Digest*, *USA Weekend*, *21st Century Science & Technology*, *The Saturday Evening Post*, *The National Enquirer*, and many other magazines. Her work has also appeared in specialized education series, websites, and promotional ad campaigns. Brenda's website: http://webtoon.com.

Check out www.worstcasescenarios.com for updates, new scenarios, and more! Because you just never know . . .

Acknowledgments

David Borgenicht would like to thank everyone who made this book possible: Jay Schaefer and Steve Mockus (you can be my nightmare bosses anytime), and everyone else at Chronicle Books; Melissa Wagner (for her stellar editing and saintly patience), and everyone else at Quirk Books; the experts who lent their knowledge and experience to the scenarios within; and of course, all the workers of the world—unite!

Josh Piven thanks all the experts who contributed their diverse range of career expertise. Without your help, writing this book would have been more work than fun.

MORE WORST-CASE SCENARIOS

The Worst-Case Scenario Survival Handbook

*The Worst-Case Scenario
Survival Handbook: Travel*

*The Worst-Case Scenario
Survival Handbook: Dating & Sex*

The Worst-Case Scenario Survival Handbook: Golf

*The Worst-Case Scenario
Survival Handbook: Holidays*

———

The Worst-Case Scenario Survival Calendar

*The Worst-Case Scenario
Daily Survival Calendar*

The Worst-Case Scenario Survival Journal

*The Worst-Case Scenario
Survival Cards: 30 Postcards*

*The Worst-Case Scenario
Dating & Sex Address Book*

*The Worst-Case Scenario
Holiday Survival Cards*